THE GLOBAL HEALTH CAREER

T0265279

The Global Health Career

A PRACTICAL GUIDE
TO FINDING
AND SUSTAINING
YOUR PLACE IN
A CHANGING FIELD

•

SHARON K. RUDY

JOHNS HOPKINS UNIVERSITY PRESS | *Baltimore*

© 2025 Johns Hopkins University Press
All rights reserved. Published 2025
Printed in the United States of America on acid-free paper
9 8 7 6 5 4 3 2 1

Johns Hopkins University Press
2715 North Charles Street
Baltimore, Maryland 21218
www.press.jhu.edu

Library of Congress Cataloging-in-Publication Data

Names: Rudy, Sharon K., 1950– author.
Title: The global health career : a practical guide to finding and sustaining your place
    in a changing field / Sharon K. Rudy.
Description: Baltimore : Johns Hopkins University Press, [2025] |
    Includes bibliographical references and index.
Identifiers: LCCN 2024042527 | ISBN 9781421450926 (paperback) |
    ISBN 9781421450933 (ebook)
Subjects: MESH: Global Health | Vocational Guidance | Career Choice
Classification: LCC RA440.9 | NLM WA 21 | DDC 362.1023—dc23/eng/20241001
LC record available at https://lccn.loc.gov/2024042527

A catalog record for this book is available from the British Library.

Special discounts are available for bulk purchases of this book. For more information,
please contact Special Sales at specialsales@jh.edu.

Contents

THE GLOBAL HEALTH CAREER

Introduction

- Why should I read this book?

Jennifer Macharia is a first-generation American health professional with roots in Ghana. She had always felt a deep interest in working internationally. Public health appealed to her because her mother was a nurse, but she was more interested in health policy, where she thought real change could occur. She had just earned a master's degree in public health and had an unexpectedly hard time getting hired. She felt frustrated and depressed about her situation and couldn't explain why she wasn't getting a job. She heard about me from her mentor and contacted me with a series of challenging questions, including, "Is my interest in a rewarding life in global health possible?" (She was sad by this time.) She asked me, "Do you know something of practical value that could benefit me?" and "How do I stand out enough to get the job I trained for?" We worked together for eight sessions. She refocused on her vision for herself and what was getting in the way. She cleaned up some distorted thinking that was creating obstacles. At the same time, we worked on her career strategy, including her poorly written résumé, feeble social media, and uninformed search practices. She mastered all the parts of a career strategy and became a confident interviewee. Fifteen years later, she checks in with me occasionally to recalibrate her career strategy and continue her rise to a significant leadership role in international development as a mission director for the US Agency for International Development (USAID), with stints in the White House as a presidential appointee. A few years ago, she asked me why I hadn't shared what I knew in writing, so I owe this book to her encouragement.

I've made a few choices in language that I would like to describe upfront. I've described groups and individuals as representing HICs (high-income countries) or LMICs (lower- and middle-income countries). The determination of whether a country is classified as a low-income country (LIC), LMIC, upper- to middle-income country (UMIC), or HIC is typically based on economic indicators, primarily the gross national income (GNI) per capita. This classification is used by international organizations like the World Bank and the World Health Organization (WHO) for analytical and policy purposes. I think these terms are less loaded than "Global North / Global South" or "developed/ developing countries." The vocabulary is challenging because its tone should be equal and respectful but understandable as a differentiating factor. I expect this contrast to shift, decrease, and diminish in unknown ways. It's also possible that there will be a much better way of describing these groups by the time or after this book is published. I hope so. I will also use the words "international development" to signify the entire universe of development, of which global health (GH) is a subset.

If you don't have time to read this book slowly, is there something new you can learn by scanning? (I'm a big scanner—often, I'll go to the chapter that seems the most useful.) I don't know if this is true for all professions, but one of the things I've loved about global health is that no matter where you are and what you are doing, you can find something that feels useful about it. From my experience and the hundreds of global health professionals I have worked with, one's professional self and work are critically important. Our careers are reflected in who we are, our values, and our identity. It's one of the reasons we put up with so much stress, working too hard, too many hours, and often have jobs that leave us constantly jet-lagged and with chronic stomach and lung issues. Our work could be linked to saving lives, no matter where we sit.

We deserve to have satisfying careers, from the first professional position to the last job before retirement, from undergraduates to postdocs, to domestically based HIC and LMIC individuals who want to work from a global lens. But maybe you are stuck and need help building the bridge from where you are now to a vision of the professional life you want. LMIC health professionals, who have typically been providers or researchers but need to think bigger about what they could achieve in this industry, may especially feel this way. You may be thinking about being a consultant or being on staff in an international organization, but why not consider leading an organization that can bid and win the most significant contracts from the most prominent donors? No matter where you are from, you will benefit from a plan that helps you negotiate your career decisions with less stress and more personal power.

A full-range career strategy addresses the classic KAP I learned at Johns Hopkins University (JHU) when doing baseline and formative research in behavior change communication—knowledge, attitude, and practice or what you know, how you feel, and what you do. I've adapted that concept for career planning so you will read about KASE, or the knowledge, attitudes, skills, and experience that contribute to the behavior of what we practice. One of the key concepts that I encourage all my clients to create is a mindset regarding their relationship with their employer. Start thinking about yourself as a "business of one." This concept is a mental posture that releases you from the unhelpful aspects of feeling attached and loyal when those feelings keep you from your own best interests. Most of us in international development gravitated to that industry because of our high value on meaningful work. You don't have to sacrifice this vital source of joy to make decisions in your best interest. A business-of-one strategy acknowledges that your organization, by its nature, will put its survival and success before any one individual.

I've worked with clients who have been fired, let go, laid off, released, faced a RIF (reduction in force), had contracts allowed to expire, or tenure denied. They were depressed and heartbroken at the deep betrayal they experienced, given how much overtime and energy above and beyond they gave to their organizations. In these situations, it is important to flip your mindset regarding your career strategy. If you're a professional, you'll share your best, but you should always keep an arm's length between you and your organization. What is the vision, mission, and strategic plan in your business of one? We'll be exploring these concepts in this book.

Your work life will shift many times as your circumstances change and your experience and expertise increase. The global workforce is shifting dramatically. Recruiters no longer make negative judgments about people who stay about two years in any position. This is now more the norm, as is changing careers. In the United States, we live thirty years longer than our great-grandparents. And more work-life balance is expected, with a greater willingness to change jobs if the environment isn't satisfying. I've included content in this book that has repeatedly proven valuable during the thirty-two years I have hired, supported, and coached HIC and LMIC professionals, helping them create their businesses of one. In this book, you will explore the mechanics of making a career strategy, a set of habits, resources, and actions that you can use repeatedly to take control of your career and move forward. Focus not just on goal setting but on goal getting. Feeling powerless, bored, frustrated, and stuck about what to do next is painful. Sometimes, people know what to do but are paralyzed and need an accountability partner. I've worked with some great coaches and learned much from them.

Who Is This Book For?

Everyone deserves a satisfying career, from the first professional position to the last job before retirement, from undergraduates to postdocs. But maybe they are stuck and need help to build the bridge from where they are now to a vision of the professional life they want. This book is also for LMIC professionals who have typically been domestically based providers or researchers but wish to tap into the extensive, more vigorous HIC resources available in international development. If you are already a global health professional, you will benefit from a plan that helps you negotiate your career decisions with less stress and more personal power.

The tent for international health careers is big enough for everyone, but people need a plan, information, and support. Here are four fictional examples and factual mashups of former clients. Do you see yourself in any of these stories?

The first client is **Heather Brown**. She is an American who recently received a master's degree in public health, an MPH. Her whole life has been devoted to mastering the academic student identity, and she's done a spectacular job. She came to me because she wanted help in developing a career plan. She didn't have a substantial professional network. Still, she had a good start by making friendly connections with fellow students and faculty she liked and respected, intern site mentors, and visiting GH professionals with whom she kept in touch and experienced mutual respect. She had already organized a few meetups, especially when people were in town. She is articulate, intelligent, and ambitious but tends to be insecure. She thinks she is harboring a secret, that she's not as great as the compliments she receives. She knows that someday, someone will find out this truth, and she will be let go, run out, or maybe never be able to get that next job. Everyone seems so much better than her. So, she's both ambitious and lacking in self-confidence. She hid it exceptionally well and was confused by how "stuck" she felt in her career planning and how stressed she was. This double dynamic has left her frightened and frozen. She knows how to be a student but feels unsure if she will do well in a professional working environment. She's in a relationship and they like to travel, but she's uncertain if her partner truly wants to live overseas if they get more serious. In a nutshell, Heather will soon be an early career professional, finishing graduate school with a history of academic success. She is articulate and appears to be self-possessed, but she feels uncertain about getting that first post-degree position.

And then there's **Jason Nguyen.** In his forties, he's already in global health and considers himself a mid/senior career professional. He has an advanced degree but is stuck and still determining the next move. He isn't satisfied with his current position but does the job well, according to his evaluations and general perceptions. He thinks his current work environment is slightly toxic, and he doesn't like his boss very much. He had always "fallen into" jobs and careers without much planning or analysis. He wants to make more money, have more authority and autonomy, and have a better quality of life. His partner, a lawyer, doesn't want to move overseas, but Jason would want to be based in the field—and his current employer trusts him enough that his work could be done mostly virtually. The challenge Jason is experiencing is being paralyzed with indecision. Should he push his partner to at least experiment with overseas living? Getting a new job sounds daunting, and he hasn't touched his résumé in years. Perhaps it's better to be safe with his current life and not risk losing what he has now. But he can't help thinking there is something else, something more that he could be doing to move up the career ladder. Jason feels stuck and bored in his current career. His current environment feels toxic or uninspiring. He is looking for something new but is unclear about what he wants and steps he needs to take. Significant considerations limit him geographically or financially, but he is looking for some stepwise strategy.

Next is **Esther Thuo.** She has been working for years based in the United States as an engineer with an MBA, but her family came from Kenya, and she wants to work there. Esther likes to understand where she came from, and after many visits yearns for her family's comfort and familiarity. She has worked in health systems in the United States and thinks she has something to offer in what has been described as "global health." But she has no global health connections and doesn't understand how it works or how to get international-level wages. Her Kenyan friends are not making that much money in Nairobi. She has traveled for her company in the past and thinks that her technical expertise would be valuable in Kenya. Esther is unsure how to get herself known to potential employers and convince them she is the right person for the job.

Joseph Manchuria is a physician in Kenya and has worked his way up in the Ministry of Health, running clinics for the past few years. He wants more impact and better access to the excellent resources and power available to LMIC health professionals who work in the HIC donor-led projects. He has developed a solid professional career but is wondering whether expanding his professional network to the HIC environment might lead to a better salary, more resources, the ability to make a more significant difference, and a path to career progression. He is still determining how to get a job in global health and how he can move from his domestic career into this work, but he sees other Africans doing it. They are getting jobs funded by foreigners and still working with other Africans. His English is fluent, but he knows it is deeply accented from a foreigner's point of view, and his English writing is a bit flawed. He's looking for a road map. He has worked with both terrible and good HIC professionals, but he strives to be patient, kind, and humble with everyone. He knows his value, and he can negotiate for what he wants. He doesn't know enough about what the negotiating points could and should be.

Ann Brown is another example of a client history I have heard more than once. Ann was a skilled, experienced senior (i.e., over the age of 50) professional whose position was cut during a reorganization. Professional life is like a pyramid: the higher you climb, the fewer positions available. But Ann had a long history of progressive promotions and success, so with her extensive professional network, she was confident that she would find something that would be a good fit without much lost time. She was able to work quickly through my steps in our coaching, so it was mysterious to both of us when no offers came. Neither of us understood the stigma she experienced as an older worker and the shock of long-term unemployment. Offer Sharone, who researches career transitions and trends at the University of Massachusetts, describes the stigma of "failure" in his book *The Stigma Trap: College-Educated, Experienced, and Long-Term Unemployed*. He discusses the complicated issues of fluctuating markets, competition, age bias, and stigma, as well as the "cruel and circular" trap in which potential employers, network contacts, friends, and spouses sometimes view the jobless with suspicion. All things being equal, employers prefer to hire the employed. Occasionally, the "unemployed" can be interpreted as "unemployable." Disciplined use of the system I'm proposing helps, but people over 50, like Ann, may need an additional set of resources based on emotional support. LifePlanningNetwork.org and AARP Foundation's "Back to Work 50-Plus" programs offer exceptional support and resources. As a coach, I have my eye out and expect more resources to be available as the preretirement global population ages.

Every single one of these examples represents things that are true about the various people I have worked with in the past. I reorganized the facts to respect people's privacy. You can probably identify something in them that fits your situation.

Why This Book Now?

More than ever, we are connected globally, even if some resist that reality. The increase in college global health programs and those considering this career makes a book like this both timely and needed. When the PHI/GHFP-II Employers' Study was published, I wrote, "What will the role of US-trained global health professionals be in the future? Where are their most likely professional positions, and how should they be prepared? Global health is an outcome and a requirement for development, security, and human rights worldwide."

All people and countries are tied together in an increasingly interdependent global health environment. This globalization, accelerated by technological advances, quickly redefines health provider roles and patient access to medical information. It profoundly influences young generations affected by the suffering they see and the personal connection they experience through the Internet. In addition, the field of global health is changing with the growing global middle-class and emerging economies. Their health needs are shifting as chronic diseases such as diabetes, stroke, and heart ailments become more prevalent, requiring attention to prevention equal to that of infectious diseases.

Furthermore, considerable government efforts with core principles of country ownership have placed expectations that reinforce countries taking charge of their health systems. In the early 2000s, many US organizations active in global health predicted this shift. They began seeking out and hiring health professionals from the LMIC to act as country directors, chiefs of party and technical directors, and entry-level staff instead of American health professionals taking those roles. Most global health professionals say this is a positive development outcome, but one result has been decreased employment opportunities for Americans overseas. Most Americans these days find global health jobs in the United States.

Another evolving reality is that most development work occurs in multi-organizational interdisciplinary groups, teams, and alliances, which require a complex set of interpersonal skills to be effective. These global, multi-country, multi-organization partnerships will continue to grow in importance even as some come and go. Current examples include Gavi, the Vaccine Alliance (an international collaboration focusing on increasing vaccine access for children in low-income countries). It works with governments, donors, and vaccine manufacturers to ensure sustainable and effective immunization programs. The Global Fund to Fight AIDS, Tuberculosis, and Malaria is a partnership among governments, civil society, and the private sector aimed at accelerating the end of the three significant epidemics: AIDS, tuberculosis, and malaria. The Coalition for Epidemic Preparedness Innovations (CEPI), an alliance that focuses on developing vaccines against emerging infectious diseases, was instrumental in the rapid development of COVID-19 vaccines. The Stop TB Partnership aims to accelerate efforts to eliminate tuberculosis (TB) as a public health problem, and the Roll Back Malaria Partnership focuses on reducing the global burden of malaria. It strengthens malaria control efforts, improves access to prevention and treatment, and mobilizes resources for malaria programs. The Global Polio Eradication Initiative (GPEI) is a partnership dedicated to eradicating polio worldwide. The Alliance for Health Policy and Systems Research promotes the generation and use of health policy and systems research to improve health systems and outcomes globally, and One Health Global Network is a collaborative approach that recognizes the interconnection between human health, animal health, and the environment. This network brings together experts and organizations to address health challenges holistically. These are current examples of the many global health coalitions operating today.

While positions were decreasing for Americans overseas, American academia discovered a significant market for global health academic programs: certifications, tracks, minors, majors, and even complete PhD programs. According to the Center for Strategic and International Studies (CSIS), a prominent think tank based in Washington, DC, comprehensive global health educational programs increased from six in 2011 to two hundred and fifty in 2016, while overseas jobs decreased for Americans and increased for LMIC professionals. According to Dr. Keith Martin, the executive director of the Consortium of Universities for Global Health (CUGH), this trend has only increased over time.

Imagine that I wrote all that in 2015, when pandemic preparedness was an interest primarily for global health professionals and Armageddon-type movies were globally successful but pure fantasy. COVID was far removed from the consciousness of policy and decision-makers. The work in the 1980s on the human immunodeficiency virus (HIV) had transformed the international development field with an influx of funding, and the aspiration of leave-behind program work was deeply embedded in the system but far from a reality. HIV had devastated LMICs, but the devastating impact of the infectious disease still was not a central aspect of HICs' daily experience. To many working in health or for anyone else paying attention, HIV taught us that country borders were useless against deadly viruses. Ebola gave us another push when it showed up in Texas. Still, COVID-19 provided life-changing challenges to the national psyche, with personal impacts and a million deaths in the United States. It has profoundly affected the heart, mind, and body. Some of us lost loved ones and our livelihoods, and many lost confidence in the future. The world changed, and with that, our sense of security. In the post-COVID world, the number of displaced persons and refugee populations with special health needs, including trauma from war, is now at our doorstep, even while battling our general malaise, polarized environments, and fear of the future.

When I was working at Johns Hopkins University, we focused on behavior change communication and worried about getting a critical mass of the end users connected through telephones, let alone computers. If a country lacked telephone poles, we knew that connecting by phone would be a challenge. Then, I started noticing people with cellphones in the most rural, isolated parts of Asian and African countries. It was a huge lesson to learn that when a capacity meets people's needs, they will adopt what works. In Thomas Friedman's book *Thank You for Being Late,* he describes the tremendous impact the Internet has had on globalization and the potential technology has to make health information accessible to anyone with a computer or cellphone. That also means misinformation, but technology has created a feeling of connection as the daily lives of other humans are revealed in all their complexity and richness in ways that we can relate to.

I call myself a "student of popular culture" because I've always been a huge television watcher, especially movies. Over the years, I loved watching American movies or television shows in any country I was in, if there were TVs in the hotel rooms. Even if they were dubbed in other languages, they comforted me, and I was proud that so many could see the American culture on display, even when it was not at its best. When I lived in East Africa, I noticed that sometimes popular American movie storylines would be reworked by Bollywood Indian companies and shown in other languages with other actors. I always felt proud that these American ideas were globally relatable. So today, as I watch television, I've noticed and love networks like Netflix, which show movies and TV series from all over the world that are amusing, entertaining, moving, and extremely popular everywhere, including in the United States. I think this will have as significant an impact on globalization as the technology itself. Humanity reveals itself in its stories, and when we identify with characters from other countries, we identify with those humans in that country. The post–baby boom generations don't know life without technology and have transformative access to cultures and the stories of others' suffering. They are connected in complex global social media chatrooms such as X (formerly Twitter), TikTok, Instagram, LinkedIn, Facebook, and the inevitable next generation of these apps. It can feel like having pen pals everywhere with whom you can communicate frequently and in real time.

When interviewing Peace Corps returnees for a research study I did in the 1980s on those who returned early, I asked about motivations. Many had been touched by and attracted to the adventure and mystery of a "more special" life. They were prompted by curiosity, having a different experience, and the warm feeling of doing good. Some just wanted to escape from a monotonous routine or were undecided about what to do next in their careers. The tech-smart generations are more informed about what it might be like but have similar motivations. That is why there has been an explosion of interest in international work. More on this in a moment. The post–baby boomers have also brought their perspective into global health work, which has affected all aspects of the work. According to Gallup, they globally demand a more explicit purpose in their work, more work-life integration, and more transparent leadership in decision making and power sharing. These groups are less willing to accept the negative aspects of work—at least for now. This shows up as less loyalty to an employer and more job movement. One thing continues, however: the value people place on their professional lives. In global health, one's professional identity is critically important. It reflects who we are, our values, and our priorities.

Why Should You Listen to Me?

When I was 14, living in rural Ohio, my father went bankrupt, and I went from having a double canopy bed in my room to sharing a bedroom with my sister in a trailer. I started working early, at age 17, because my family needed the money. With that history, being independent and able to earn was an emotional given I considered a survival priority. I worked through school and eventually accumulated a master's degree, a specialist in education degree (EdS, a year after a master's), and a PhD, which I earned while working full-time in my forties. The degrees still operate as a security blanket and source of pride.

I was just so happy to have a job. I didn't negotiate salary in my early career because I didn't want to scare anyone off. After my senior college year as an exchange student in The Netherlands, I worked for a few years trying out different business environments—a Dutch Johnson's Wax factory (still the most exhausting job I've ever done), retail, a law office, organizing private parties as an assistant to the food and beverage director of the Breakers Hotel in Palm Beach, Florida, the office manager of a Yacht Brokerage House (it was Palm Beach, after all). I've been a salesperson, lifeguard, factory worker, restaurant hostess, secretary, administrative assistant, private party organizer, and office manager.

After a few years of postbaccalaureate jobs, I returned to the University of Florida to study counseling. Eventually, I got a job as a counselor in an international high school exchange program. I ultimately became the director of participant services, working in Europe, South America, and Asia, specifically Japan, where I did my dissertation research studying the strategies people use to adjust to change when adapting to new cultures. During this period, I was very focused on cross-cultural communication and adaptation as well as training and counseling. After fourteen years of outstanding performance evaluations, I was topped out, exhausted but stuck. I didn't want the next job up, but I just couldn't let go of the familiar. This was my tribe! Then,

I lost a political battle and was fired. I was devastated, but it was the best thing to happen to me. I was frozen in a job that no longer met my needs, but I was horrified at the idea of job hunting, which I found overwhelming and stressful.

Because I had a lot of training and counseling experience, I consulted in Africa for the Johns Hopkins Bloomberg School of Public Health's Center for Communication Programs. A friend I had made attending the American Counseling Association's annual conference worked there and recommended me for a consultancy. After several successful consultancies, I was hired as a senior program officer to work in Africa, attending to the center's focus: social and behavior change communication. I came to JHU in midcareer and was clueless about global health's business and technical aspects. But I knew international work, training, and counseling. I spent six years in Africa and have remained deeply grateful to many African nurses who taught me how things work in their world. This job is where I first began learning about the business of global health and the complicated role of HIC donors and academia in the industry. Did I mention that I'm terrible at learning new languages? Thankfully not being fluent in multiple languages has never been a dealbreaker.

I worked for JHU Bloomberg School of Public Health designing, implementing, and evaluating national behavior change communication and client–provider interaction interventions in many technical health areas and with various end users. I was lucky that JHU's Center for Communication Programs (CCP) had a potent combination of program implementation and academic research cultures. Changing careers took work, however, and academia's competitiveness and unrealistic expectations often beat me. I am rarely able to respond in the moment, but I recall one job change interaction that I found deeply satisfying. I was in an elevator with the founder and director of the program. She was brilliant but prickly, and I had had a few run-ins with her. In this instance, she said, "Most people tell me that they regret leaving CCP." I responded, "No, they just tell you that." That was when my business-of-one identity was conceived, and I felt a shackle fall to the floor. I soon left the organization for a leadership position at IntraHealth in North Carolina.

I was "headhunted" to work with IntraHealth, a global health nongovernmental organization, then embedded in the Medical School at the University of North Carolina in Chapel Hill, North Carolina. It was career advancement and a better technical fit—training and human performance improvement. By this time, I was paying much more attention to my gifts and work preferences. While there, I was the technical director and then deputy director of USAID/Global Health Bureau's flagship performance improvement and training projects. This is where I learned much more about development politics and working with donors, and I became more adept at proposal and grant writing. I was recruited to clean up a messy situation in a hostile work environment. I connected with like-minded people who remained good friends and helped me learn from various management mistakes and victories.

I also learned the importance of articulating the value of what I bring to any organization. I was doing a long-term project at WHO in Geneva. The chief executive officer of the Public Health Institute called me about a new position in Washington, DC, a project director position overseeing a just-won fellowship program, which would have meant advancement. The job was perfect for me. I wanted the work and knew the value I would bring to it. Yet I was willing, without resentment, to walk away if I didn't feel right about the entire compensation package. He offered me the position without an in-person interview and gave me what I requested. Over the years, I have become better at understanding my strengths and weaknesses. I love being part of a team or an organization, but I had learned to put myself first and not fall head over heels in love with any organization. In the end, I knew it would be unrequited. I want you to benefit from what I learned so that your business of one can be fully equipped to trust the decisions you make—without the stress of regret or later resentment.

I was the project director for a series of USAID's flagship global health fellowship programs (Population Leadership Program, Global

Health Fellows Program 1 and 2) for the Public Health Institute with the US government's secret security clearance for the next twenty years. I focused on building the next generation of global health professionals and supporting GH professionals' professional and organizational development within the USAID system. A few thousand early/mid/senior career professionals went through the fellowship programs, which were two- to four-year full-time positions as nondirect hires in the USAID system in Washington, DC, in the missions, and at various organizations throughout the world, including foundations and international NGOs like the United Nations Development Programme (UNDP) and WHO in Geneva.

I was proud that over 40 percent of fellows were LMIC professionals. To work in a USAID Washington, DC, or mission office, you need security clearance, which requires permanent residency status or US citizenship. I was always proud of my secret security clearance, even though I was advised not to include it on my résumé so people would not think I was a spy for the Central Intelligence Agency (CIA). I led or was a senior writer for several successful multimillion-dollar proposals during this period, and I have been a significant contributor to more than a billion dollars in contracts and cooperative agreements.

Entering the global health/international development environment when I was already midcareer was challenging but ultimately advantageous. I maintained an observer's point of view, and many of these observations come from already being a seasoned professional. This slightly removed stance is one of the reasons that I've accumulated wisdom that has been helpful to my clients. My inner observer was on high alert. I learned how the global health business works and how to identify and express the value I bring to my workplace. I want you to benefit from what I learned so you can be fully equipped to trust your decisions—without the stress of regret or second-guessing yourself.

Early in my career, I became a board-certified counselor and later a board-certified coach. I eventually became a published researcher and author. Before COVID and the Great Resignation in the United States, I completed part-time work with the Public Health Institute. I had already learned to trust the universe more and focus on what value my experiences might have for others. I created TeamRudy LLC, a private coaching and consulting organization with corporate and nonprofit organizations and personal coaching clients. I developed this book to share what I've learned about getting into this industry and thriving in global health careers.

What Questions Will Be Addressed in Each Chapter?

Introduction

- Why should you read this book?
- What are some typical career dilemmas faced by job-hunting global health professionals?
- Why should you listen to me?
- Why are global health careers so popular now?
- What are some of the career challenges?
- What is the author's story and credentials in this area?
- How does this book intend to address them? How is the book organized?

Part I. Big-Picture Considerations

Chapter 1. Global Health Definitions and Locally Led Development

- What is the global health landscape from a career perspective?
- What are the implications of the localization or decolonizing movement for my professional life?

Chapter 2. Key Competencies in Global Health

- What key competencies do I need to be successful in global health?

Chapter 3. Career Considerations across the Lifespan

- What primary global health career paths could I take, and what preparation matters?

- How do I move from a domestic to a global health position?
- Are there special considerations based on where I am in my professional life?
- What are the challenges of transitioning from being a student to a professional?
- Can a senior-level professional benefit from career planning?

Part II. Building the Foundation

Chapter 4. Building the Foundation by Knowing Where You Are Now

- What's the best first step in my career-planning process?
- How can using mindfulness techniques, the awake inner observer, and self-reflection help me build the foundation for my career strategy?

Chapter 5. Creating the Vision

- Why is creating a vision of my future professional self so important?
- How do I create a clear picture of myself in the global health professional life I want?
- What is a stepwise process to turn my vision into doable goals?

Chapter 6. Identifying the Gaps

- What steps can I use to analyze all the information I've collected to identify critical, bridgeable gaps between where I am now and where I want to go?
- How do I uncover the gaps in my knowledge, attitudes, skills, and experience that get in the way of my vision for my professional life?
- How can I identify outdated thoughts, ensuring my thinking supports my goals rather than limiting them and, ultimately, my success?

Chapter 7. Goal Setting

- What stepwise process can I use to create goals that plug the gaps I've identified while working toward my vision?

Part III. Goal Getting: Implementing the Plan

Chapter 8. Creating Your Professional Records System

- What paperwork filing system can I create to make life easier as my career progresses?
- What's the latest in what works in résumés and cover letters?

Chapter 9. Your Online Presence

- Do I need to use social media in my business-of-one concept, and which platform is most used by recruiters?
- What are the best practices for creating a LinkedIn profile that stands out to recruiters and headhunters?
- Which are the leading Internet sites where employers post positions?

Chapter 10. Creating a Professional Networking System That Keeps on Giving

- Is networking an essential aspect of strategic career planning?
- Is it possible to foster natural networking that doesn't feel manipulative or awkward?
- How do you plan networking opportunities, establish professional relationships, and ensure mutual benefit?

Chapter 11. Interacting with Potential Employers and Coworkers

- What is the informational interview, and how can I ace it?
- What are the best practices regarding the pre-interview, the interview, and post-interview communications?
- What are some considerations when deciding if the position is the right fit and negotiating the entire package?

Part IV. Becoming a Lifelong Career Strategist

Chapter 12. Putting It All Together with New Mindsets and Habits

- What is this process in a nutshell?
- What's next?

Appendixes

- Turning an Unintentional Thought into an Intentional One
- Global Health and International Development Job Websites
- Résumé Template

PART I

BIG-PICTURE CONSIDERATIONS

CHAPTER 1

Global Health Definitions and Locally Led Development

- What is the global health landscape from a career perspective?
- What are the implications of the localization or decolonizing movement for my professional life?

If you are an American, it is easier to get a job working in Kenya if you already have overseas work experience. That is, unless you have valuable technical or practical experience. In this book, I share some strategies for early and midcareer professionals to get around these roadblocks. In this post-COVID world, we are expanding traditional explanations based on what professionals seek when discussing global health careers.

In this chapter, I explore the current thinking and propose an expanded term. You'll notice that I don't use the term "international health." Nor will I quibble about such variations—I leave that to the academics who love to splice terms. Instead, like the World Health Organization, I primarily use "global health" to describe the work and the field it represents. It is a more inclusive term that encompasses not only the health issues that cross international borders but also the interconnectedness of health issues, their impact on populations worldwide, and the need for global cooperation to address them. As used in the past, the term international health often implied a focus on health issues specific to international borders or foreign aid efforts. In contrast, global health reflects a more modern understanding of health challenges that transcend national boundaries and involve factors such as globalization, climate change, emerging infectious diseases, and health disparities that affect people worldwide. I'll throw in "planetary health," "one world health," or any other term that reflects the critical interconnectedness of the earth, its weather, and its organisms, including humankind.

Robert Kaplan, a former professor of epidemiology and global health at the University of California, Los Angeles (UCLA), and his colleagues defined global health as follows: "Global health is an area for study, research, and practice that places a priority on improving health and achieving equity in health for all people worldwide. Global health emphasizes transnational health issues, determinants, and solutions; involves many disciplines within and beyond the health sciences and promotes interdisciplinary collaboration; and is a synthesis of population-based prevention with individual-level clinical care."

More recently, the Lancet Global Health Commission on High-Quality Health Systems in the SDG Era defined global health as "an area of study, research, and practice that prioritizes improving health and achieving equity in health for all people worldwide. It emphasizes health systems, policy, and governance, focusing on health's social, economic, and environmental determinants." The Consortium of Universities for Global Health (CUGH) defines global health as "an area for study, research, and practice that prioritizes improving health and achieving equity in health for all people worldwide. Global health is a multidisciplinary field that encompasses a range of global health issues, including communicable and non-communicable diseases, health systems, environmental health, and social determinants of health."

All these essential definitions by major international organizations focus on improving health and achieving equity for all people worldwide. And they share little that would help someone prepare to do global health work. I agree with and appreciate the "we-are-all-connected" reality, sensibility, and state of mind, but it doesn't serve us as job hunters. Having a "one health" perspective won't get you a job, let alone a career in global health. As an alternative, I suggest this definition to start the discussion: "Global health is a multifaceted field that centers on enhancing health and striving for health equity on a global scale. It encompasses various disciplines, addresses all health-related issues, and its business practices are firmly grounded in economic dynamics and relationships among high-income, middle-income, and low-income nations."

Let's look at these examples:

A. If you are a Kenyan working for a European Union–funded health project in Nairobi, are you working in global health?
B. If you are an American doing your practicum or internship in a predominantly refugee community in an American city suburb, are you working in global health?
C. If you are an American doing your practicum or internship in a low-resource inner-city community, are you working in global health?
D. If you are a Kenyan health professional working in the state of Minnesota, are you doing global health?

By most current definitions, yes, you are doing global health work. Yet employers told us that when they see the experience described in items B and C on résumés, which they often report seeing, they *do not* count them as global health experience. For A and D, employers don't even question whether your work is global health because, for them, you have already checked that box by being from an LMIC.

Think of global health as a business that includes strategies, goals, resources, predominantly donor funding, and many politics. For example, the funder/donor is critical in setting the agenda. This could be a foundation like Gates, a government entity like USAID, or a country's Ministry of Health. This role should not be underestimated. Understanding how the funder thinks, their priorities, and preferred ways of working are often only learned on the job and yet are critical to successful global health work. We need to take it seriously and teach what the practical reality of the work is, how priorities are decided, how the resources flow, and how decisions are currently made. Along these lines is tracking the growing influence of corporations and how market forces and business interests are increasingly shaping global health. Some think the commercialization of health is a worldwide trend, and one could point to the role of the private sector in shaping health policy, research, service delivery, and practice around the world. Private sector involvement in global health can bring benefits, such as innovation and efficiency, but also risks, such as conflicts of interest, lack of accountability, and the potential for profit to override a country's public health goals. While you debate this topic, consider the new interest and global health professionals needed to support corporations and their foundations as they enter international development to do good and make their mark. With their resources, you could help influence the impact of market forces on health equity, social justice, and human rights.

The donors, whether government or private, use various experts to create long- and short-term strategies that they fund primarily through competitively bid contracts or grants. The donor sets the plan and the evaluation criteria by which success is judged. Donors tend to favor those organizations that share their nationality, and historically, much funding circulates through the donor/implementer system, staying in HICs. This is being explored now through the lens of localization, to be discussed later.

Donors develop strategies and write solicitations. Other organizations then write proposals, letters of intent, or other project documents. These are usually competitively bid, but only sometimes. Think of the *Hunger Games* book series, where only one, the "prime," is left standing after violent competition. Donors have widely varying degrees of involvement in implementation and requirements for evaluation. USAID is the largest international development donor in the world at the time of this writing, though the Gates Foundation is also a major global health donor. They work with experts (many of the funders themselves with expertise) to create big strategies and partner as best they can with LMICs. As of this writing, www.workingforUSAID.gov is USAID's laudatory effort to involve new types of partners. It is also an introduction to the vast bureaucracy and the effort it takes to tap into those resources. USAID is also accountable to Congress, the White House, and the American taxpayer, which can often be heavily focused on how international health supports homeland security and safety, so various agendas heavily influence priorities and accountability. Another donor group is the emerging powerhouse of global alliances, some of which I listed in the introduction.

One of the problems I see is that the visions of HICs and LMICs are too limited. For example, in the capacity-building project I worked on previously, an American company was an equal partner with two well-respected African clinical research institutes. The donor wanted to build capacity by strengthening the research skills of African clinical researchers. We asked for what purpose. So they could be good consultants for HIC organizations (academic, corporations, nongovernmental organizations, for-profits, not-for-profits, etc.)? We proposed that the donor think more strategically. If they wanted to build sustainable capacity, why not create interventions that gave clinical researchers the knowledge, attitudes, and skills to run their institutes and be competitive bidders against the HIC organizations? So, we proposed to add two areas to the research-focused Health Expertise competency category: Development Practice and Interpersonal Effectiveness. These competency clusters will be explored further in chapter 2.

Locally Led Development

Besides deciding on a meaningful definition, let's explore another big-picture topic, because your opinions will influence your career decisions. Exploring global health as a broad topic should also include locally led development, which is picking up steam as I write this book.

Locally led development has always been a highly valued concept (the old "we work ourselves out of a job" concept). It's also one that we have consistently failed to achieve. Many of our development systems support something different. The idea began as capacity building, then we started to hear about decolonizing, then localization, and now we've landed on "locally led development." USAID, which is valiantly struggling to realize its vision on this, defines locally led development as "the process in which locally led actors—encompassing individuals, communities, networks, organizations, private entities, and governments—set their agendas, develop solutions, and bring the capacity, leadership, and resources to make those solutions a reality." It's currently considered a key strategy essential for scaling up and sustainability.

Billions of dollars have been spent on international development, a substantial amount cycling back to the HICs through the contracting process. With most projects, including local capacity building, evaluated as successful, it's frustrating that significant change often doesn't last. The explorations and attempts to address these issues have profoundly affected the work. But success stories (checking back ten or twenty years later) are still not the norm when describing local capacity development and sustainability initiatives.

This complex reality and the energy focused on making changes are crucial considerations for any global health professional. Suppose we are to do well in this profession and be satisfied with our investment in this work. In that case, we must understand the historical implications that influence the work and our contribution. We can either be part of the problem or the solution. It starts with your understanding and tracking the fast-evolving focus.

The challenges we are facing in international development are rooted in its history. Indigenous communities have had their knowledge and practices regarding health for thousands of years. Healing was embedded in the social system with natural remedies and different ways of understanding the body, health, disease, and healing. In the 1600s, there was a perfect union between "HIC" missionaries and their governments. With their mutual desire for expansion came the imposition of Western values and systems onto colonized societies.

Yes, there were incredible, significant contributions of science and the scientific method, but with all that came the medical model, which mainly focused on the physical body. With the medical model, health and illness were viewed primarily through a biomedical lens rather than considering social, psychological, environmental, or political determinants. The model focused on diagnosis, treatment, and managing diseases and conditions mainly through medical interventions. HIC missionaries and colonists also brought specialization and expertise, the hierarchy of care, a focus on disease prevention, and the licensing/hierarchy of practitioners with them to these countries new to them. Sound familiar?

All of this was entwined with the HICs' colonial agenda. At one point, malaria was seen as the single greatest challenge to expansion because it was killing colonists. Writings of that period, which have been traditionally hidden, are now resurfacing in which the relationship between the colonizing process and medicine was glorified.

HIC academic researchers and clinicians jumped on the opportunity to work in impoverished, low-tech settings with high disease burdens. This work was considered a professional knowledge-generating opportunity to be exploited, which Westerners did. The writing of those times revealed that most of HIC academia felt impoverished low-tech settings with high disease burdens were research havens, and that included neither respect for Indigenous health systems nor respect for the population that they experimented upon. For many academics, it was not about helping but about publishing. For example, it was standard practice to keep findings private from those in-country professionals involved in the research.

Robert Horton, editor of the *Lancet*, has written some gut-wrenching editorials on this. He said, "Medicine and global health continue to be entangled with colonial attitudes, structures, and practices—from scientific journals to research funders, how health services are provided and who can provide them." Wrapped in all of that were good works. Still, there was also violence, brutality, slavery, and many writings on the subhuman qualities of the Indigenous population. In other words, we "othered" the LMIC population.

Yes, many heartfelt, well-meaning, and significant contributions were made during this development era. Still, we also must own the power differential, abuse, and disrespect for differences as the roots from which international development grew. Even now, most of the money goes from HIC governments to HIC organizations, and many rules and regulations support this closed system. HIC experts learned to lead with the solution because "Isn't it our role to fix things?" Our job has been to deliver solutions, which was our way of helping and what we were paid to do. Almost every solicitation contained the desired solution embedded within it.

To complete the picture a bit more, we also must acknowledge the part-stereotype, part-truth of the LMIC environment, which historically has had poor accountability for financials, program interventions, and evaluation results. Stories of local and government corruption have been shared and stored. We have all been equally guilty of favoring our bureaucracy, hierarchies, and tribes.

Slowly moving toward change has been a twenty-year process. After the 2005 Paris Declaration, HIC organizations that were active in development started changing their country office staff from HIC nations to LMIC or local professionals. As I write this, an intense global conversation occurs on two fronts: (1) the flawed nature of the international development process and (2) the inequities and the chronic power differential between the HICs and LMICs that contributes to the lack of successful development.

Two key issues have kept us from the vision of global health, which seems so easy to imagine but is challenging to implement. One is accountability; HIC citizens expect their governments and organizations to ensure resources are well spent and that LMICs can implement and evaluate interventions according to donor standards. This lack of trust in LMIC organizations to handle leadership and the infrastructure necessary to manage money and resources and report back has required HICs to work in ways that diminish autonomy. Technology has profoundly affected the ability to access critical data and information that allows anyone to judge the quality and impact of activities. All of this has been hampered by the corruption that has plagued the LMIC government health systems, which is hard to identify and address.

Five necessary conditions then developed, which set the scene for the possibility of something closer to locally led development, or the decolonization of international development. These are:

1. The Internet, technology, and globalization connected us in ways never seen before. In his book *Thank You for Being Late: An Optimist's Guide to Thriving in the Age of Accelerations*, Thomas Friedman makes the point in many ways that the Internet has blown up traditional knowledge hierarchies and their limited access. He shares multiple examples of how technology has connected us as we share our stories and make knowledge, including health information, accessible to the remotest regions and anyone with a connected cellphone.

2. Pandemics amplified HICs' self-interest in LMIC health. The AIDS global pandemic led to the rise of billions of dollars being invested, as well as large, complex international alliances involving multiple countries. Pandemics caught the attention of the HIC population, which began to understand the disrespect bacteria and viruses have for national borders. This led to intense interest in global health as a safety and security issue for the HICs that felt vulnerable and suddenly at risk. COVID-19 traumatized the entire international system.

3. A critical mass of trained, highly competent LMIC health professionals. Because training was the easiest capacity-building intervention and well within the comfort zone of HIC organizations and academia, international development unwittingly eventually created a critical mass of LMIC health professionals who had developed outstanding technical and programmatic expertise, leadership acumen, and a mind of their own.

4. LMIC health professional activism. That cadre of LMIC technical experts started leading their institutes, doing their research, and showing up on panels and in print, demanding equity,

starting with publication credit. They then moved quickly into the exploration of resource inequities. They were the first to start pushing back against the practice of LMIC researchers receiving no credit in research publications, and lopsided allotment of the donor's financial resources with HIC partners receiving more than the lion's share.

5. Insufficient sustainable change, thus decreasing impact. International development has saved millions and millions of lives and helped countless people. Yet, despite the millions of lives saved through the President's Emergency Plan for AIDS Relief (PEPFAR) and other initiatives, we continue the ritual of anxiously waiting for congressional reauthorization and other HIC foundation and government approvals.

There has been a shocking lack of continuing, sustained change and permanent impact when factoring in the decades and vast amounts of human and financial resources that HICs have invested in development. Because we now had decades of data, we saw that billions spent could have produced actual capacity, sustainability, or permanent scale-up. The lack of permanent solutions created by most projects were still evaluated as successful, and the increasing frequency of this story set the scene for locally led development as a possible solution.

With the growing momentum within the international development community for a fundamental reset of business as usual, USAID, to their credit, decided to take this issue on. They invested in staff and made locally led development a strategic priority. Their first lesson was that they were a big part of the problem and were not going to meet their initial goals. Their complex procurement system, which favored the large implementing partners and their risk aversion, were significant obstacles to change.

In 2023, they began tackling risk and accountability, program implementation, relationships with local partners, staffing, and culture. This involved building two-way trust with regional partners who reported needing more capacity to address procurement challenges, reporting and compliance issues, and insufficient funding.

USAID staff started working directly with local partners, which has meant a diminishing role for the implementing partner. This has stretched USAID's staff capacity, which also must manage the administration and oversight of fieldwork for the federal government. They may yearn to be field implementers. But their leading the labor-intensive co-creation activities with local partners, program management redesign, and significant new evaluation systems are probably not a workable, long-term solution. They can't do this alone and need other donors and seasoned experts to support the work.

Some solutions they are experimenting with include paying local organizations for their co-creation time, making it easier to submit unsolicited bids. They are also considering paying 20 percent overhead costs. (This is a significant change from the past's 0–5 percent overhead costs but may differ from some implementing partners with much higher overhead costs approved by the government.) However, it is still far from the MacArthur Foundation's 28 percent level of effort to local organizations. The donor is also experimenting with creating truly descriptive solicitations rather than prescriptive and aggressively hiring local community representatives and technical experts.

The charitable giving of MacKenzie Scott, the former wife of Jeff Bezos, has made significant impacts not just because of the dollar amounts but also her approach. Since her divorce in 2019, Scott has donated over $17 billion to more than 2,300 nonprofit organizations across various sectors, including education, racial equity, LGBTQ+ rights, and global health. Her approach is notable for its "no-strings-attached" methodology, allowing recipients to use the funds as they see fit, which has been highly praised for its effectiveness and efficiency in addressing urgent needs. Scott's donations are detailed on her website, Yield Giving, which also outlines her process of conducting private and anonymous evaluations of potential recipient organizations to avoid burdening them with the application process. Scott's philanthropy has been described as transformative, with recipients reporting profoundly positive effects on their operations and capabilities.

As USAID reflects on how to make its systems and approaches more local user-friendly, they are also focusing on teaching local organizations how to work with them. There has been mutual accountability in evaluation methodologies, especially participatory methods, data management, privacy, and how to share and use results. As they engage in listening tours, a co-creation process for new programming, streamlined accountability systems, and participatory evaluation, they are beginning to struggle with this work's deeper, unconscious, underlying elements, including:

1. Context. A deep understanding of the environment where the end user lives is critical because health is shaped by the environment—complex politics and local social fabric.

2. Who is the expert? HIC knowledge hierarchies have traditionally excluded LMIC public health providers and relegated them to stakeholders or implementers who are consulted but not engaged. Personally, this is where I learned not to use a banana to demonstrate how to use a condom in family planning counseling unless I clearly stated the banana was meant to represent a man's penis. There is this persistent old-school idea that providers can't be experts.

3. The importance of lived experience when choosing local representatives. There are a lot of research teams whose engagement can remain on the surface with communities directly affected by the research issue, so when selecting local partners, make sure the organization can bring the context, knowledge, and lived experience. Don't assume the headquarters office of an international NGO is representative. Homentum's research reports that local representatives of international NGOs complain that their leadership doesn't listen, and the rest of the work doesn't challenge that, so create more autonomy for locals to lead the

development agenda, and don't assume international NGOs are genuinely representative.

4. People's capacity is a strategic lever of change. Locals' work depends on their human and resource capacity. Their ability to work is adversely affected by limited funding and inadequate coverage of operational costs. Opposing funding access and conditionalities does not support equitable and locally driven development.

What has helped us reach this crucial point is the critical mass of LMIC health professionals who have the personal capacity and knowledge to lead considerable efforts. Over the years, I have never worked on a USAID, United Nations, or Gates-funded project that didn't feature capacity building and sustainability. Training LMIC health professionals has often been embedded in any USAID project, and this has borne fruit over the years.

With technical leadership competence and the technology that allows for sharing information and accountability, we are now at a critical point of shifting significant power from the HICs to the LMICs. One other dynamic is crucial in true partnerships, however, and that is our concept of who the other is. Whether framed as racism, colonialism, or cultural stereotypes, this lack of respect and trust has been systemically woven into structures in both the HICs and LMICs.

Two serious obstacles have prevented the vision from being substantially realized. One of these obstacles has been accountability. Organizations and their donors are often beholden to their government supporters and, ultimately, the HIC populations for the funding entrusted to them. This has resulted in a set of requirements and oversight that has impeded the level of risk and true partnership that would be requirements for localizing global health work. The second obstacle has been the human dynamic of being safe and secure by accumulating and keeping power. Fundamentally, switching roles with the HIC in a supportive role and the LMIC leading the way in goal setting, strategy design, and implementation reflects a willingness to give away resources. That "willingness" state can only happen if reinforced by the environment, from training to employment expectations and rewards.

Besides a critical mass of universally respected LMIC health professionals, technologies have been advancing that ensure resources are appropriately accounted for, research is implemented correctly, and the program is on course and well done. These technical systems, which can now be part of global self-organization, decrease the oversight and travel traditionally required when an HIC donor provides resources. Improved program and funding tracking systems, plus a critical mass of trained, competent LMIC professionals, have led to a crucial moment in international development.

The critical area of localization or reimagining the business of global health is a vital part of current development practice. This will be a significant future trend as we experiment with various strategies. The goal of localization is to move decision making and implementation as close as possible to the end user. This includes dealing with calcified structures and our humanity's worst and best aspects. Being awake and conscious of the hidden dynamics will help you navigate the global health industry as part of your career planning. Everyone in the future will be either contributing to the status quo or helping to change the inequitable system that became historically entrenched because of power, greed, and misplaced religiosity.

Whatever culture or country you identify with, while the points of suffering exist within the LMIC, the entire structure of international development is premised on the HIC's perceptions. Both public and private donors, who are the primary source of resources, have most of the power and authority and dominate how relationships are defined with the LMIC, where the end user and the work are.

When working in Tanzania, I remember that every donor's solicitation expected the responding proposal to include local capacity development, yet external donors funded 96% of the national health system. That level of dependency is both crippling and enticing. Developing sustainability is authentically aspirational for many individuals I have worked with. But the culture and the implementation systems remain resistant to change.

I chose two big topics for this introductory chapter: (1) emphasizing the "business" of global health in its definition; and (2) locally led development. They are priorities because of their evolving and profound impact on our professional lives. You will limit your global health success if you focus only on the health or technical content of the work and ignore how business is done in this industry. Where do you situate yourself in the system? What compromises do you consider reasonable and practical, and what role could you play in moving the needle forward on localization, if you truly believe it's the right way to go?

Various realities have successfully prevented or continually weakened a sustainable vision of an independent or at least competitive LMIC. Change is happening, however, to make LMIC organizations more independent. This includes prioritizing LMIC organizations' technological infrastructure to manage, monitor, and report on funding, program implementation, and results. But there is a vast difference between believing in the decentralization of power and actually letting go. Academia, please consider going beyond case studies and include experiential learning approaches that will help new global health professionals become more adept with whatever end of the power-sharing role they work in. Whatever your nationality, having a deep awareness of the complexities of power giving, receiving, and sharing and aligning that awareness with your behavior is key. It will create an internal consistency within yourself and result in your being more effective in whatever global role you have.

CHAPTER 2

Key Competencies in Global Health

- What key competencies do I need to be successful in global health?

During the years I directed global health fellowship programs for USAID, I was the official legal supervisor of a few thousand early- to senior-career global health professionals. My team was responsible for recruiting, hiring, supporting, and evaluating their performance over the two to four years or more they worked full-time within the USAID system in the United States and overseas. During those years, I sometimes had to terminate someone's employment. It is the meeting that most employers dread.

I felt great compassion for these individuals as I sat with them and delivered the "this fellowship is not a good fit" or "you have not been able to resolve the challenges that we outlined in your performance improvement plan" message. Most often, they were stunned, reminded me of their documented history of career success, and described an honest confusion and frustration with what had happened. They could not master the behaviors they needed to be successful in the USAID context and were often in shock at such a significant first-time failure. Many were physicians or PhDs with a long history of being admired for their deep technical knowledge. Collaboration, communication, or team membership difficulties were the most common reasons they were fired. I had personal experience with the dynamic of being terminated, so because of that painful lesson, I strove to avoid the anger and disappointment that protect a supervisor from the discomfort of delivering painful news. Not everyone is able or willing to negotiate complicated interpersonal team memberships, alliances, and intricate collaborations, which are the key ways of doing business in USAID. I took pride in the fellowship's ability to call out these failures in ways that were hopefully non-shaming and to vigorously support behavior change. If all interventions fail, managers must let that person go with empathy, clarity, and support for their next professional steps.

In this chapter, I'd like to share my experience, what the research tells us, and what my employees have taught me about what one must master to be a successful global health professional. An ongoing discussion in global health in the United States centers on the future of the US-trained global health workforce and how best to prepare all professionals for this career path. I have previously mentioned the spectacular growth of academic global health programs—from complete PhD programs to GH tracks and certifications—that exploded throughout the 2000s. In recent years, global health professionals and academics in the United States have devoted considerable effort to developing competencies for international health programs to encourage rigor and consistency across programs. There are a variety of competencies and competency models related to global health. If you are lucky, your university team used some of those to develop curricula.

I told most of my story in the introduction, but to be more specific for this chapter, my first foray into global health competencies occurred as a worldwide health implementing partner, first as the technical director and then as the associate/deputy director for the USAID GH Bureau's flagship global health performance improvement and training project (PRIME I and PRIME II). I was a member of the 2014–15 Consortium of Universities for Global Health (CUGH) subcommittee, which created the competency material used by CUGH, published the 2017

Employers Study, and participated in the 2020 STAR competency documentation, all noted in the Further Reading section. I've made many presentations on this subject at USAID, the Centers for Disease Control and Prevention (CDC), American Public Health Association (APHA), Homentum (a global organization offering operational and program learning), GH Council (GHC), and CUGH and have received invitations to speak at several universities. I recently served on an advisory group for Northwestern University's master of science in global health (MSGH) curricula review. In this chapter, I won't be using the typical competency matrix. Though I value the work done to create those frameworks and their contribution to academia in developing curricula, I prefer to cover the high points with a slightly different flavor from the global health work world—the employers, including myself, and the job hunters. Professional growth and mastery come from experience and executing either research, program implementation, or direct service provision (more details in chap. 3).

After implementing and evaluating competency frameworks in several programs, I started thinking about broader categories led by the learners and focusing on performance. An employer's priority is your performance. Knowledge and attitude are contributing factors, but behavior is everything. Competency programs often evaluate mastery appropriately but may fail to capture salient competencies. The challenges I experienced trying to work with competencies as an employer could be sorted in six ways. (1) The process of developing competencies leads to an unwieldy, hard-to-manage number. (2) It's hard to decide what matters for each person because positions are constantly evolving and everyone's career path is unique to them. (3) A learning program, based on competencies, tends to cater to the most minimal skill level. (4) We often teach people what they already know. (5) The program overly focused on competency mastery tends to focus on the test or whatever measure is chosen. (6) All the learning doesn't necessarily ensure good job results. This is especially true for those competency systems that emphasize learning over performance. Competency systems fail when someone officially "masters" the competency but fails in their work.

The CUGH's Competency Subcommittee's project developed a list of eighty-two interprofessional competencies in twelve domains. We started with more than six hundred competencies, and the activity led to more questions about the future of global health work for new graduates with a master of public health (MPH), as well as global health programs and domestic worldwide HIC, MIC, and LMIC health professionals who want to move into global health work.

Since then, every project I have worked on has included some competency-creating process, and almost everyone struggled to maintain its relevance in our VUCA (volatile, uncertain, complex, and ambiguous) work environment. With all the complications of competencies, you can get overwhelmed. But I can show you a more straightforward way to look at things.

In this chapter, I want to talk about the knowledge, skills, and experiences as well as attitude areas as a guide for global health career strategists to pay attention to their strengths and potential gaps but not to measure those topics in any way beyond their ability to discuss them intelligently and to work in positions that require from "familiarity-with" up to "expertise-in."

In Global Health Fellows Program II, we used the competencies sparingly, mainly as a self-assessment tool both pre- and post-fellowship. The fellows measured themselves in five competency groups.

I. Health Expertise (they filled in the blanks as they each were working in different health areas)
II. Process and Resource Optimization (funding mechanisms, strategy development, organizational dynamics, project management, implementation science)
III. Professional Capacity (written and verbal communication, analysis and problem solving, workplace norms and behavior, prioritization, and self-management)
IV. Interpersonal Effectiveness (cultural understanding, flexibility, adaptability, collaboration and teamwork, initiative, creativity, change management)

V. Knowledge Management (continuous learning, information processing, systems thinking, capacity building, development context)

In each of the five competency clusters, they selected where they currently were in their proficiency levels using this list:

1. awareness, observer, or neophyte
2. acquiring, learner, or novice
3. developing, contributor, or apprentice
4. intermediate, practitioner, or journeyman
5. advanced, expert, or guru

The fellows' most common answers for Health Expertise, Professional Capacity, and Interpersonal Effectiveness were 3 and 4. So, they thought they had some mastery of these content areas, which remained consistent pre- and post-survey. The most common responses for the Process and Resource Optimization and Interpersonal Effectiveness were neophyte and novice (1 and 2). No one ever rated themselves as experts (5) on anything, even the very senior fellows. We called these fellows USTAs (uniquely qualified senior technical advisors) and were able to pay them outside the regular USAID salary ranges because of the flexibility of a cooperative agreement. This was one way we got very senior, already-established talent into the agency. Post-fellowship, although everyone moved forward in almost every area, the most significant change was in Process and Resource Optimization (II), where people appreciated how much they learned about global health business by working inside the donor.

So, let's walk through four areas: knowledge, attitudes, behavior, and experience. I've sorted the need-to-know content into four topics or competency clusters:

- health expertise
- the business of global health
- intrapersonal and interpersonal effectiveness
- technology, including knowledge management

First Competency Cluster: Health Expertise

According to the World Health Organization, cardiovascular diseases, cancer, and respiratory disease are the leading causes of death worldwide. But what kills most people in lower- and middle-income countries are contagious or infectious diseases, maternal and child health issues, and noncommunicable, chronic diseases, primarily because of limited access to health care and poor living conditions. Cardiovascular disease, cancer, and diabetes are becoming more prevalent as lifestyles change and people adopt more sedentary lifestyles and eat unhealthy diets. So, there are countless ways to organize health expertise topics to address what kills the most people, even while considering quality-of-life issues. In considering the competency cluster of health expertise, we can look at three areas: health domain or topics, technical capabilities, and populations.

Regarding the health domain, academic knowledge is the most accessible, foundational beginning of global health competence. In the Employers' Study, 85 percent of global health employers surveyed agreed or strongly agreed that academia could better prepare students in nonclinical (everything except health expertise) skills—what the work is. The respondents thought academia does well when helping students master the scientific or clinical aspects of health, such as technical health knowledge. Examples of health domains include biostatistics, environmental health sciences, epidemiology, health policy and management, and social and behavioral sciences, which are often sorted this way in MPH curricula. Health topics also include infectious diseases with HIV and other pandemics, malaria and tuberculosis, "neglected diseases" (meaning diseases that are unpopular with the big funders), reproductive health including demographic expertise, health systems, and nutrition, as the main examples.

Technical capabilities can also be expanded into areas such as health and environment, humanitarian assistance and disaster mitigation, education, agriculture and food security, animal life, water, environmental effects, energy, urbanization, economic growth, and significant crisis/conflict/instability as well as democracy, human rights, and governance. Oh yes, there is health and humanities, social sciences, animals, and the one-world content that combines the health of the planet, the animals, and people. See what I mean? The connections between health and other content are endless and constantly evolving.

Populations are also a significant health domain competency focus, and specific populations can be a valuable career focus. You can have a rewarding career by concentrating on many groups whose support and betterment feel personally meaningful. Everyone is represented in the lifespan, from infants to the elderly. Humans can also be sorted by citizenship, ethnicity, race, class, wealth, education, gender, gender identity, and sexual preference; professions such as policymakers, community health workers, sex workers, pharmacists, nurses, or physicians. Also, consider those with chronic or terminal diseases; additionally, consider the displaced, breastfeeding mothers, and people of various body type, disability, marital status, or career or education. As many ways as you can sort human beings into groups, you can identify populations segmented into end user groups, all of which can be an important focus of research and intervention. A few groups are stable in terms of funding for research and implementation, so it is easy to create careers around them, such as vulnerable populations like infants, mothers, youth, and people at high risk for infectious diseases. An additional growing group is people who have had experiences, including home or on-the-road accidents, trauma, and survivors of events like war and natural disasters that led to displacement. You can also track global trends tied to global security, such as pandemics, food insecurity, climate change–related health issues, and displacement as a result of war or famine.

You can use these three complex health expertise competency areas (health domain, technical capabilities, or populations) as foci of self-reflection. For example, when reviewing all the vulnerable populations, consider if any group calls to you or seems particularly meaningful or exciting. You can then focus on gaining experience and expertise with this population. In later chapters, I'll discuss the "awake inner observer" and the importance of noticing and assessing what attracts you in health-related areas. For example, one client I worked with was a brilliant midcareer researcher who had a disability that required him to walk with a cane. Early in his career, he decided to "wall off" that part of his reality because he felt it would diminish his professional success. When we started exploring his vision and "why," it became clear to him that his disability was an important, valuable part of his identity and that factoring that into his professional vision would make his work more exciting and rewarding. He quickly became an expert on this topic and is now thriving, doing work that reflects all of who he is in the best way possible.

My experience running learning programs led me to be more critical of standard competency global health formats typical in academia that tend to focus on the science of health-specific topics. Instead, when I have spoken and written on global health competencies, I've learned to look at the topic from a career point of view. What are the areas that, taken together, allow one to survive, thrive, and succeed in the industry? Whenever I talk about health topics as competencies in global health, I see the expectations on the faces of those who think this is all they need to know. And why not? This way of thinking has been emphasized in academia, whose members often have decades-old field experience or are researchers not interested in applying their findings. Teaching experimental design is perfectly acceptable if that is your personal solid preference. But it can't replace program design and implementation if that is your preferred focus.

Health expertise is necessary but only part of the story if you want to succeed. So, I will lay out the prominent trends in various categories of competencies and help you view these as a career strategist. You can decide whether you envision yourself in research or program design. In this chapter, we'll also explore some of those common threads.

If you are interested in laboratory research, for example, you would want to know about health science, designing and planning ethical research, protocol operations, data flow, research operations, study, and site management. An excellent researcher also knows how to pay attention to initiating and closing studies, reporting status, and interacting with the public. They value and understand how to communicate lessons learned to community partners and global constituencies while exhibiting cross-cultural communication skills that demonstrate respect for other perspectives, populations, and health care systems, that is, cultural understanding.

Second Competency Cluster: The Business of Global Health (Development Practice)

Global health business does not figure largely in academia. Yet employers value the knowledge, attitudes, skills, and experiences of this sector (remember the Employers' Study?). We tend to neglect how the business works in early career training. Understanding what global health is and why people are trying to reimagine it is also often neglected but critical when considering career planning. I think this category is so crucial that in 2022, I proposed it as one of three key competency categories for a project funded by PEPFAR and USAID to build capacity for African clinical researchers. We often leave people to figure out the critical roles of various players in development, how funding and resources flow, and how to engage in sustainable, scaled-up systems. We should start with the larger vision of global health and be honest about how and why this work gets done. Then, you decide what part you want to understand, master, and influence.

Focusing on the business of global health as a competency area, consider reviewing the following list and decide where you are on the neophyte-to-guru span.

Attracting funding and optimizing resources

- Writing successful contract/grant proposals tailored to the selected donor
- Negotiating for resources and publication credit
- Budgeting for research studies, programs, and organizations
- Mastering budgeting and accountability practices

Donor and partner relations

- Identifying donor and funding sources
- Engaging funding sources
- Explaining how funding mechanisms work by the donor
- Identifying and engaging partners, including prime and subcontractor roles
- Becoming the preferred subcontractor or prime (trust, accountability)

Organizational capacity strengthening

- Identifying and implementing internal financial systems that use technology to ensure transparency and accountability
- Designing sustainable workforce development strategies
- Identifying methods for assuring health program sustainability
- Assessing existing capacity
- Developing strategies that strengthen community capabilities for overcoming barriers to health and well-being

Sociocultural and political awareness

- Understanding the roles and relationships of the entities influencing global health
- Analyzing the impact of transnational movements on health
- Knowing the context-specific policymaking processes that impact health
- Describing multiagency policymaking in response to complex health emergencies
- Understanding the interrelationship of foreign policy and health diplomacy

Strategic thinking

- Tracking global trends and opportunities
- Understanding locally led development (localization, decolonizing, reimagining) GH strategies

- Developing a business case
- Connecting research results to policy and programs
- Identifying the relationships among patterns of morbidity, mortality, and disability with demographic and other factors in shaping the circumstances of the population of a specified community, country, or region
- Mastering context-specific implementation strategies for scaling up best-practice interventions

Ethical reasoning and professional practice

- Applying fundamental principles of international standards for protecting human subjects in diverse cultural settings
- Analyzing the distribution of resources to meet the health needs of marginalized/vulnerable groups
- Understanding ethical and professional issues in responding to public health emergencies
- Explaining the mechanisms to hold international organizations accountable for public health practice standards
- Promoting integrity in professional practice

Project management skills

- Leading and motivating a project team toward completing a project
- Communicating effectively (including regularly) with team members, stakeholders, and clients to ensure everyone is on the same page and understands the project goals and objectives
- Planning and scheduling a comprehensive project plan that includes timelines, milestones, and deliverables, as well as managing and adjusting the plan as needed throughout the project
- Identifying potential risks, developing strategies to mitigate them, and managing and responding to unforeseen risks as they arise

- Managing project budgets and resources effectively, including overseeing costs, allocating resources, and tracking expenses
- Ensuring quality standards, including those of project deliverables and that the project meets or exceeds client expectations
- Identifying and solving problems that arise during a project and making effective decisions when faced with uncertainty or ambiguity
- Working effectively with team members, stakeholders, and clients and fostering a collaborative and productive working environment
- Demonstrating flexibility and resilience to changing project requirements or circumstances, especially when facing unforeseen challenges or obstacles

There are significant disadvantages to the short-term, quick-results, donor-driven project culture that permeates how global health work is done. To advance in this work culture, you must become adept at baseline and formative assessment as the foundation for one- to five-year designed, implemented, and evaluated projects. I've noticed that professionals trained in the project-driven environment of global health tend to do well if they decide to work domestically. This observation is supported by research. *Harvard Business Review* (*HBR*) published an article in 2023 indicating that projects have displaced operations as the economic engine of our times: "By 2027, some 88 million people worldwide are likely to be working in project management, and the value of project-oriented economic activity will have reached $20 trillion." *HBR* invited companies to reinvent their approach to general management and adopt a project-driven organizational structure.

These competencies are all interrelated and critical for successful project management. Developing these competencies through training, experience, and ongoing learning can help project managers lead their teams and deliver successful projects.

Third Competency Cluster: Intrapersonal and Interpersonal Effectiveness

This is a critically important competency cluster and the most common cause of failure to succeed. As mentioned previously, challenges in this area were a frequent reason for failure to grow in the global health programs I oversaw, specifically in two critical scenarios. One was the inability of the fellow (an embedded contractor) to work in a team, and the other was being unable to get along with their government bosses. Mastering this competency is a continuing process of becoming a functional member of a highly complex, interconnected environment and subtle, complicated alliances that involve different ages, genders, cultures, religions, and technical areas. Sometimes, the fundamental dynamic is the clash between an unhealthy manager lacking in a few critical interpersonal skills but more empowered than the fellow. If the fellow could not find a way to work with the manager, the fellow lost the struggle, given that the manager was the more powerful government employee. This territory also reflects professional capabilities and is best viewed from a self-assessment perspective.

The following are critical aspects of intrapersonal and interpersonal effectiveness.

Collaboration and teamwork

- Building trusting partnerships
- Being an influential team member
- Maintaining a robust professional network
- Developing procedures for managing partnerships
- Facilitating and participating effectively in meetings
- Promoting the inclusion of representatives of diverse constituencies in partnerships
- Using diplomacy and conflict-resolution strategies with partners and staff

Communication

- Listening skills
- Sharing lessons learned with community partners and global constituencies
- Demonstrating respect for other perspectives (including that of donors), populations, cultures, and health care systems (cultural acumen)
- Public speaking
- For researchers, study communications include:

  1. Initiating and closing studies
  2. Reporting status
  3. Interacting with the public and research participants

Leadership

- Creating and aligning vision
- Influencing and coordinating group actions, including managing organizational change
- Mastering the self and encouraging others

Management

- Designing work plans
- Understanding technology-based financial systems and budgets, focusing on transparency and accountability
- Recruiting, supporting the performance of others, and ensuring retention of valuable staff
- Creating and delivering training
- Supervising and mentoring, including effectively delegating
- Overseeing subcontractors and consultants
- Managing the impact of knowledge management initiatives on organizational processes and workflows, including addressing resistance to change, facilitating smooth transitions, and aligning knowledge management with strategic objectives

Professional writing

- Proposals for grants and contracts
- Technical publication
- Emails, correspondence, blogs, opinion articles, and letters to the editor intended for business purposes or for the public

Mindfulness

A critical area of intrapersonal effectiveness is mindfulness, including emotional intelligence. From a career strategy point of view, mindfulness can be defined as a state of focused attention and awareness that enables individuals to perform their work tasks more effectively and with greater clarity. It involves being fully present in the moment, without judgment, and with a heightened self-awareness and emotional regulation. Why should mindfulness be an essential aspect of your professional life? It can be a valuable tool for career strategy. It enables you to approach your work with greater focus, clarity, and well-being, ultimately leading to greater career success and satisfaction. Suppose you've ever felt victimized by a senior professional known for their angry rants, cruel remarks, or unhelpful emotional outbursts. In that case, you've witnessed poor self-management skills that ultimately can hurt people's careers. Mindfulness techniques can help with the following.

- Improve your productivity. By cultivating a focused and clear-minded approach, mindfulness can help you prioritize your work tasks and increase efficiency.
- Enhance your communication skills. Mindfulness can help you to be more present and attentive when communicating with others, improving your ability to understand and connect with colleagues, clients, and stakeholders. It also helps you manage your reactivity so you never say or email things you wish you could take back or live to regret later.
- Manage stress and burnout. Mindfulness practices can help you manage stress better, reduce burnout, and maintain your

overall well-being, which is critical for long-term career success.

- Develop leadership skills. Mindfulness can help you develop greater emotional intelligence, empathy, and self-awareness, critical attributes for effective leadership.

Several competencies are involved in mindfulness, and they can vary depending on the specific model or approach to mindfulness. Here are some of the most cited competencies.

1. Regulating attention is sustaining attention on a chosen object or task and disengaging from distractions.
2. Being aware without judgment or able to observe experiences, thoughts, and emotions without evaluating them as good or bad.
3. Being aware of your thoughts, emotions, and bodily sensations in the present moment.
4. Being able to extend compassion, kindness, care, and support to oneself and others.
5. Being curious by approaching experiences with inquiry and an open attitude, without preconceptions or biases.
6. Accepting experiences as they are without trying to change or resist them.
7. Regulating emotions, especially negative ones, skillfully.
8. Acting intentionally and with purpose based on one's values and goals.

Fourth Competency Cluster: Technology and Knowledge Management

"The knowledge, innovative technologies, and proven tools to help millions of needy people are within reach. Yet, a wide gap remains between what can be done with existing knowledge and what is being done" (WHO 2002).

Technology is influencing our worldview in profound ways. It has fueled globalization and connected the world, and many young people who have never traveled have experienced personal connection through social media and the Internet. The role of technology has evolved as a significant driver of globalization, and its importance is showing up in all aspects of development work, including access to learning and health care. In *Thank You for Being Late*, Thomas Friedman discusses the potential of technology to improve global health outcomes:

> Thanks to technology, we are on the cusp of a revolution in health care, which could finally shift the emphasis from treating sickness to creating wellness. We can now sequence the human genome and use that knowledge to create personalized medical treatments. We can use data analytics to identify patterns and predictors of disease and to develop more targeted and effective interventions. And we can use telemedicine and mobile health technologies to deliver care to people in remote or underserved areas and to empower patients to manage their health.

We will also use artificial intelligence (AI) to potentiate all that technology offers, so this is a critical competency area for global health professionals.

At Johns Hopkins in the 1990s, we needed help figuring out how to use landline phone systems in LMIC communities to unite groups and improve emergency health systems. We soon noticed people walking around and talking on cellphones in the most isolated areas of low-income countries. The technology changed lightning-fast, and the early adopters took it on. It was driven by end users choosing a solution that was accessible, affordable, and worked for them. "Leapfrogging" refers to a critical mass quickly adopting newer and more advanced technologies rather than investing in older technologies that seem less efficient or effective. In LMIC areas, where the infrastructure for older technologies might not exist, it was much easier and more cost-effective to adopt newer technologies to meet their needs even better. Still, it meant understanding that the countries' technology histories could and should be different, with LMICs getting the best and latest whenever possible.

Another example of the emerging importance of technology in global health careers has been the shifting nature of positions in monitoring and evaluation. Many fellows in the Global Health Fellows Program (GHFP) at all levels have been embedded within PEPFAR since its inception. I was there initially and co-facilitated the first ambassador-level meeting in Africa. But that's another story. What started happening in PEPFAR is that, over time, PEPFAR faced bigger and bigger multiple data streams that needed to be organized and connected, but PEPFAR was unsure how to do that. Anyone with a big-data systems skill set quickly became one of the most sought-after professionals in the HIV/AIDS community because there was so much pain in the organization around managing the various data streams to make sense of it and uncover its hidden gems.

Technology is also influencing early career professionals. In a 2019 study through CUGH, we examined the job search employment experiences and job availability of current global health-focused master's level graduates. The study sample included students graduating with master's degrees in global health, public health with a global health concentration, or global medicine from eight US universities. One hundred and fifty-two people completed the survey, with 102 (67 percent) employed. Of unemployed graduates, 38 percent were currently in another educational program. Out of 91 employed respondents, 67% reported they had limitations or gaps in their academic training. Besides project management and proposal design, one of the gaps was the types of technology and software they were familiar with and could use. This occurred in both job descriptions and during interviews.

As an aside, the majority of employed respondents reported they currently worked in North America (83.5 percent); however, only 31 percent reported the desire to work in North America after graduation. Employers needed professionals who knew not only data analysis software and systems but also data visualization software and techniques. Of course, all the software that is part of communicating, holding complex virtual meetings, storing data, and working virtually was requested. It surprised the job seekers and was identified as something they wished they had learned in school.

As I write this, concepts like blockchain, AI, and the metaverse are coming into the global health world. Anyone with experience and an educated point of view regarding the use of technology in global health will have an advantage career-wise. Also, LMICs are learning to use the latest technology to track and report on funding and programming, a significant requirement for a successful locally led development.

The final point in the technology competency cluster is related to knowledge management (KM). I've integrated a discussion into this section because, although there are other aspects of KM, including interpersonal communication, there are critical technological tools to support this activity. One commonly referenced concept is the "knowledge doubling time," which represents the time it takes to double the total amount of human knowledge. This idea was first proposed by Buckminster Fuller, a futurist and inventor, in the 1980s. According to some estimates, the knowledge-doubling time was around fifteen hundred years in the early eighteenth century. In the 1980s, Fuller estimated that human knowledge doubled every twenty-five years. It is believed to be as short as six to eighteen months in specific fields today. Information overload isn't a feeling; it's the result.

The advent of the Internet and digital technologies has played a significant role in accelerating knowledge growth. It has made information more accessible, facilitated global collaboration, and rapidly disseminated research findings. Additionally, fields such as artificial intelligence, genomics, nanotechnology, and other emerging areas are experiencing remarkably rapid growth, pushing the boundaries of knowledge even further.

So, what do we do with all the information pouring in? While knowledge is expanding quickly, our ability to fully comprehend and apply that knowledge to real-world challenges may still need to catch up. Integrating and practically utilizing new learning can take time, and ethical, social, and policy implications of certain advancements may require careful consideration.

Knowledge management competencies, the skills and abilities required to manage and utilize knowledge within an organization effectively, include the following.

1. Information technology proficiency. Using knowledge management tools, software, and technologies. This includes understanding and leveraging technologies like content management systems, collaboration platforms, data analytics, and artificial intelligence.

2. Continuous learning. Committing to personal and professional growth and staying updated with the latest trends and developments in knowledge management. This includes a willingness to learn new techniques, tools, and methodologies. What are the key websites and organizations you have tagged, regularly scanned, and are trusted to give you the latest and best curated accurate data and trends?

3. Analytical and critical thinking. Analyzing and evaluating knowledge to identify patterns, trends, and insights. This involves critical thinking skills, data analysis, and the ability to draw meaningful conclusions from information. With all the data coming in, what is valuable and what is not?

4. Knowledge capture and documentation. Identifying, capturing, and documenting knowledge from various sources, such as experts, documents, and databases. This involves techniques like interviews, surveys, and knowledge mapping. It also includes your ability to select and track the best websites for global health information relevant to your career path, such as Academia.edu to track your publications. This is also how you keep ahead of career-making trends and where the jobs are. Follow the money and your passion. This competency also helps you keep up with the workflow while keeping sight of the big picture, the longer-term results, and the outcomes or intended achievements of your work.

5. Knowledge sharing and collaboration. Facilitating the exchange and sharing of knowledge among individuals and teams. This includes creating platforms for collaboration, fostering a knowledge-sharing culture, and implementing tools and technologies to support sharing. Do you know how to use Zoom? Teams?

6. Knowledge storage and retrieval. Managing repositories and databases, organizing information in a structured manner, and implementing effective search and retrieval mechanisms. This involves categorization, indexing, and metadata tagging. In another way, this competency also includes managing your calendar and your "to-do" list so you can get things done, one day at a time, but also keep your work in its place and not at the grocery store, where we should have our food list, not our work list, on our minds.

7. Knowledge transfer and training. Facilitating knowledge transfer from experienced individuals to novices within the organization. This includes mentoring programs, onboarding processes, and training initiatives to ensure knowledge is effectively passed on. You may not be the trainer, but you need to know the best, most efficient transfer techniques—as both a recipient and provider of the knowledge.

8. Knowledge creation and innovation. Encouraging the generation of new knowledge and fostering a culture of innovation. This involves promoting idea generation, supporting experimentation, and providing resources for research and development. This is a core principle in international development.

Many researchers believe their job is done when a peer-reviewed article is accepted for publication and perhaps shared at a conference. They created new knowledge, and it was time to follow their curiosity and create more understanding with the subsequent study. This is an entirely acceptable and valuable career focus.

Part of knowledge management that focuses on how information flows down from research to on-the-ground professionals (think a medical director of a clinic in Mombasa) and how information on creative local solutions flows up to more people, perhaps in another part of the world. An interesting career option—knowledge management expert—has developed as a result of the frustration experienced when one notices needed solutions (evidence-based best practices) that seem unknown to the medical director of that Mombasa clinic or when we stumble upon innovative solutions designed locally that have tremendous implications for communities in another part of the world. The entire info system can seem like one big traffic jam. Wanting to understand how knowledge moves through the system led a small group to develop the Implementing Best Practices Consortium, now the Best Practices Network, overseen by WHO and funded by USAID, with more than 147 member organizations (www.IPBNetwork.org). I'm proud to say that I was part of that early group of thinkers, frustrated by the obstacles of knowledge flow and an early developer of the IBP Network along, with Dr. Jim Shelton and the entire MAQ (Maximizing Access and Quality) team at USAID as well as Maggie Usher-Patel and others at WHO.

In this chapter, I used a competency approach to describe the areas of mastery you can utilize to self-assess and decide what is important to you. Consider these four competency clusters plus the intrapersonal competency of mindfulness as you test these ideas: health expertise, the business of global health, intrapersonal and interpersonal effectiveness, and technology and knowledge management. Whether you are looking for graduate programs, your next or last global health position before retirement, or you've already retired and are thinking about focusing only on activities that reflect your gifts and your interests, this chapter will help you concentrate on those masteries that matter to you and support strategic career moves.

CHAPTER 3

Career Considerations across the Lifespan

- What primary global health career paths could I take, and what preparation matters?
- How do I move from a domestic to a global health position?
- Are there special considerations based on where I am in my professional life?
- What are the challenges of transitioning from being a student to a professional?
- Can a senior career professional benefit from career planning?

In my first global health job, I was in my late thirties with no experience in health or developing countries. I had plenty of overseas experience, a PhD, and deep expertise in counseling and training, especially across cultures. Johns Hopkins University hired me because of that expertise, but I didn't know much about how global health worked. That I had already lived overseas twice seemed to check the employer's box for international experience. Still, I'm not sure I would have counted those comfortable countries—Japan and The Netherlands— in the same way I value the experience I subsequently had living in Africa. Because I was midcareer, I came in as a senior program officer, jumping over all the super-smart program officers with master's degrees in public health. JHU wanted me to help with the "interpersonal communication" part of the Center for Communication Programs, and I eventually developed expertise regarding client–provider interaction. JHU/CCP staff were generous with their knowledge. Still, I didn't have the technical expertise in reproductive health, infectious disease, maternal/child health, or health systems, nor did I understand the business of global health. I had much to learn about donors, governments, academia, companies, and where local communities and end users stood in this complex system of goal setting and resource allocation. In my first assignment, my Ghanaian boss sent me to help CAFS (the Council for African Family Studies) redesign their six-week communication program in Kenya. CAFS staff were already communication experts, so I could bring value in updating their training system and the client–provider interaction training, but it was a trial by fire.

I believe that experience so many years ago helped me be a better career coach because I learned quickly how much my technical expertise was hampered by what I didn't know about the industry. I understood one professional system but had substantial knowledge gaps in other areas relevant to global health. The first obstacle I faced was that I did not understand the layout of the global health landscape, detailed in chapter 1.

Another big obstacle is that I didn't know anyone in global health. I had no professional network in worldwide health and only a distant relationship with US State Department staff—nothing with USAID, my major donor, nor WHO or health-focused foundations. When most people talk about the United States' external-facing focus, they mean the "three-stool" approach—one stool requiring three legs to keep its balance—of diplomacy, defense, and development. I was most familiar with the State Department and diplomacy because international exchange work was housed in that agency. I had some familiarity with defense, the second leg of the stool, because family members were career military. But I was no more informed than the average citizen regarding development. Previously, I talked about the competencies needed. In this chapter, I am exploring the different paths one can take to get into development.

Let's explore GH career planning further throughout one's lifespan, with a variance in emphasis if you primarily identify as being from an HIC or an LMIC. I've included a discussion of the type of degrees that can fit comfortably under the global health umbrella and whether a medical or direct service provider degree and experience are necessary. No matter where you are in your professional life, your planning will have unique considerations depending on where you are in the lifespan. We will explore professional themes and factors from early-, mid-, and late-career strategies and aspects of transitioning midcareer into global health from a domestic career, whether you are an HIC or LMIC professional.

The good news is that global health needs just about any expertise you can imagine. Almost any experience is valuable if the timing and situation are right. Over the years, the Global Health Fellows Program hired veterinarians and veterans, linguists and lawyers, engineers and ecologists; we hired geographers, psychologists, sociologists, anthropologists, scientists of all kinds, educators and trainers, communication and social media experts, organizational development experts, business professionals, information and computer technologists, and all sorts of direct service providers including a variety of registered dieticians, dentists, physician and nurse specialties, and counselors, among many other disciplines.

In global health, there are three primary career paths: direct service provision, research, and program implementation. You can, and people often do, thread in and out of these areas, but spending an entire career implementing one path is also appropriate. Understanding these choices is essential in early career planning because, especially in the beginning, each path requires unique expertise. Although overlapping in some technical areas, each path involves specialized knowledge, attitudes, and skills. The more you understand, the easier it will be for you to focus your preparation, whether you are considering entry, reinforcing what you already want to do, or thinking about making a switch. Isn't it wonderful to have various career tracks while building depth in the global health arena? The combinations of technical foci, end user identities, cultures, and skill combinations are almost infinite.

Career Path 1: Direct Service

The first career stream is that of providing direct service. This means that you are a health provider in some manner. Special training, certifications, or licensing—such as a medical, nursing, counseling, physical therapy, health site administration, laboratory work, nutrition, dental, or pharmacy degree—is typically required.

As I mentioned previously, the concept of specialization in health provision is one of those big assumptions we transported along with our religions and culture as we colonized and created international development traditions. This traditional way of understanding health has only lately led us to a greater awareness of the social and political determinants of health and the profound truth that the most significant health provider in the world is the mother. If direct service is your personal vision, then paying attention is strategic because degrees, certifications, and licenses are still substantial and typically central requirements.

An advanced degree, especially a doctor of medicine (MD), is still one of the most common routes for an LMIC professional to expand into the international development community. Their direct service experience can be valuable if they see how their work fits into a more extensive health system. This contrasts with the preponderance of HIC professionals who do not have direct service experience but often have public health training or another technical area of expertise that has proven relevant and valuable. As I noted in chapter 1, if one looks at the history of international development, in those early days and even now, there is a focus on Western healing and definitions of health, and the domination of medical doctors as the exclusive experts led to bringing those tendencies or that focus into LMIC schools of medicine, nursing, dentistry, and pharmacy as the way to prepare for a global health career.

Mostly, a health professional dedicated to direct service is either part of an organization embedded within a country's health system like Doctors Without Borders or working in refugee, humanitarian, or conflict zones. The abundance of LMIC physicians in international development is a legacy of how this business started and what was favored and valued by the HIC donors, governments, and academia. For an HIC professional from any discipline, there is a legitimate path to direct service provision in LMIC environments. Moving to and attempting to get a position within the country's health system is complicated by each country's rules, and work permits have become more difficult to obtain over the years. The following organizations are not the only ones; others could be excellent, but these are the ones I've come across over the years that impressed me as providing valuable experiences for direct service providers.

1. Peace Corps. This is a well-known volunteer organization. Volunteers usually serve for twenty-seven months, which includes training and service in the host country. It's a unique opportunity for Americans to live and work in communities abroad. The Peace Corps Response Program offers limited opportunities for direct service short-term activities. Global health employers also widely accepted the Peace Corps as a sufficient overseas living and working experience.

2. Doctors Without Borders / Médecins Sans Frontières. MSF is an international medical humanitarian organization that provides medical care and assistance to people affected by armed conflict, epidemics, natural disasters, and exclusion from health care. They recruit medical professionals, including doctors, nurses, and other health care workers, to work in their programs worldwide.

3. International Medical Corps. A global humanitarian organization that provides health care training and medical relief to communities affected by conflict, natural disasters, and poverty. They have programs in more than thirty countries and recruit medical professionals to work in their programs.

4. Partners in Health. A global health organization that works to bring high-quality health care to underserved communities worldwide. They recruit medical professionals to work in their programs in Haiti, Lesotho, Liberia, Malawi, Mexico, Peru, Rwanda, and Sierra Leone.

5. Health Volunteers Overseas. A nonprofit organization that aims to improve health care access and quality in LMIC countries by training and supporting health care professionals. They recruit medical volunteers to educate and train health care workers in their partner countries.

6. Seed Global Health. A nonprofit organization that aims to strengthen health systems in resource-limited settings by training and supporting health care professionals. They recruit medical professionals, including doctors, nurses, and midwives, to work in their programs in sub-Saharan Africa.

Within the direct service career stream, there is concern regarding using LMIC sites for HIC medical students to "practice" their skills. Jessica Evert, medical director of Child Family Health International and former faculty at the University of California, San Francisco, and others have led these discussions regarding the complex dynamic of medical students practicing or experimenting in LMIC environments in ways they would never be allowed to do in their medical schools or local communities. Consider staying with the better-known, respected organizations previously noted, and be particularly cautious when considering privately led small groups.

The first stream of global health careers—direct service provision—is probably the smallest group. It can be satisfying for those who are called to that work and love working directly with patients and clients. It also provides a direct experience of the health provision system, though I can't help thinking that the end user, the client, or the patient is the voice that should be loudest in our work.

Career Path 2: Research and Evaluation

The second GH career stream is research. Researchers create new knowledge. They move information an inch, sometimes a mile, down the road. The focus is creating hypotheses, developing new products, doing laboratory work, collecting data, performing analysis, writing reports, publishing, and perhaps public speaking. These positions are often in academia but also include donors, corporations, and not-for-profits, and the territory is complex and evolving. I'm including evaluation in this category because the skills needed to set up monitoring and evaluation systems require similar knowledge, attitudes, and abilities, as described in chapter 2.

The complexity of technology's evolving contribution to this career stream is significant because of its fast pace and immediate utility. For example, the Global Health Fellows Program I and II hired many data analysts for the President's Emergency Plan for AIDS Relief from the beginning, but the needs became more complex over time. In PEPFAR, the amount of data coming in was overwhelming, and it was a severe challenge to connect and make sense of a variety of different, massive data streams from various countries, government agencies, and organizations coming into the centralized office. So, we started looking to hire those experienced in "big" data analysis and the use of the new technologies to not only organize multiple streams of massive data files but also to pull meaning and conclusions from them and create exciting visuals to illustrate the results that would make sense to and be compelling to nonscientists. In the 2019 article, "Employment Opportunities and Experiences among Recent Master's-Level Global Health Graduates" (hereinafter called the Recent Grad Study), we followed 152 recent MPH/MSH graduates in their job search. They reported surprise at how many employers wanted to know what software they could manage—management, operations, research, presentation—all kinds of software. The respondents identified this as one of the skills they wish they had learned in graduate school.

I've discussed the related competencies in this territory in chapter 2, but from a career-planning viewpoint, consider the attitudes that might make this path attractive to you personally. Great evaluators, like great researchers, are driven by deep curiosity about the truth of a situation. They are relentless in their pursuit of the facts. The best ones know how to remove themselves from the desire to reach certain conclusions, especially those desired or expected by the donor and implementers, and search for the story that the facts tell. Could you be as excited to find out you were wrong about something because you found the more accurate and correct cause? They don't fear surprise and are willing to be taken by the unexpected. They recognize and immediately reject groupthink, even if it means being unpopular. Monitoring and evaluation (M&E) are career paths that have remained marketable and easy to transport across various disciplines. Almost all donors expect their investments to be evaluated, and they want someone other than the implementers to do it, even if the M&E specialist is a team member. It's also a career with a lot of flexibility, with competent persons becoming high-profile consultants for those who don't want or can't afford full-time M&E staff. The best M&E consultants are there from the beginning of a project design, creating the evaluation systems they will use to judge the results of any intervention.

Just as the direct service provision requires a rigorous training process, research requires an academic learning environment. Whether it's scientific, medical, laboratory, social science, participatory, or process research, there are a set of principles that you must learn and often credentials that are useful for career entry and advancement. The dark side of research is the pressure that many academics experience to show evidence of original published scholarship. This "publish or perish" mindset has created a glut of information that is often incremental or minor, and the volume of studies and the number of publications, especially now with online capabilities, make it almost impossible to keep up and to identify valuable results. There is also an increasing cost to getting something published that creates an additional obstacle to those who have an important story but not the funds to cover the publication costs some journals are now demanding. Search engines, AI, and meta-analyses can help you ensure knowledge management is one of your critical competencies. If you find joy in satisfying your curiosity about how things work, research is a beautiful, rewarding global health career. If you are more interested in creating impact, perhaps based on research results, consider implementation as a career path.

Career Path 3: Implementation

Implementation is the process of carrying out something planned or decided. It includes analyzing and defining a problem and its background, selecting goals, choosing target audiences, staffing the work, creating the work plan, and determining how the work is financed and done. Since I started working in global health in the early 1990s, these programs have typically included some capacity and sustainability development expectations. They also include attention to DEIA (diversity, equity, inclusion, and accessibility). Today, you can study implementation as a researcher. It's called "implementation science," a multidisciplinary field focused on bridging the gap between research findings and their practical application in real-world settings. It seeks to understand the processes, strategies, and factors that influence the successful integration of evidence-based interventions, programs, and policies into health care systems and other sectors. The primary goals of implementation science include the following.

1. Translating research into practice. It aims to facilitate the effective and efficient translation of research discoveries into practical, everyday use. This can include implementing new health care treatments, interventions, or policies.

2. Improving quality and effectiveness. Implementation science helps identify the best practices for implementing evidence-based interventions, focusing on enhancing the quality and effectiveness of services or programs.

3. Addressing barriers and challenges. Researchers in this field study the barriers and challenges that can hinder the successful implementation of innovations. They work to find solutions to overcome these obstacles.

4. Evaluating impact. Implementation science also involves assessing the impact of implemented interventions to determine their success, adjusting as necessary to achieve desired outcomes.

5. Scaling up. Besides individual implementation, it often explores strategies for scaling up successful interventions to reach larger populations or broader geographic areas.

But don't get confused. Studying implementation science is *not* the same as being an implementer. Implementers are right in the middle of all the complex work, having to consider the human factor at all levels. Another word for "implementation" is "execution." Both terms refer to putting a plan, idea, project, or strategy into action or practice. Locally led development is expected to have the most impact on this career path. For now, however, I don't foresee large shifts but the inclusion of more human-centered practices and inclusive program design, implementation, and evaluation.

Walking through health competencies, I described many areas of health expertise and end users. What would you add today? In localization, the process starts with co-creating with end users, with local actors leading the way. But no matter how many types of interventions or end users, donors continue to want some history of the problem and previous interventions, a description of the target audience and interventions, a work plan, and a monitoring/evaluation plan. Along with the project plan is the budget and justification for the resources that will be needed. Donors always need a story that they can document and share with others. This has been the consistent core approach to project development for government agencies such as USAID, foundations such as Gates, and international organizations such as the UN system, including WHO. Such agencies are by far the most popular stream for global health professionals.

You can have a career that includes all three of these themes, but I've differentiated them because the technical requirements that allow you to work prominently in each of these streams are different. Some are overlapping, but there are some unique requirements that I've described in this book. If you are already in a graduate program, there are some things that you can do now to balance out your résumé and skills acquisition. I've suggested a few items in chapter 6.

Thinking about Graduate School?

What kind of degree is most important? Is it necessary to become a doctor or registered nurse? Is a master's degree enough, or do you need a PhD? Well, it depends on the work you want to do. Because of the medical model roots of international development, there is still a powerful bias toward MDs in direct service and PhDs in research. In the third career path, implementation, there is more flexibility depending on the technical area. I found less flexibility regarding career choices with MDs until I sought specialized development training. Suppose someone wants to get into the work as quickly as possible. In such cases, MPH, MHS, or other master's degrees have the best applicability and flexibility across many technical areas. You can get a position in global health with just a bachelor's degree, but you will hit a ceiling quickly as you compete against people with advanced degrees. The truth is that any degree can work depending on what employers seek, and their needs are eclectic and varying. As I mentioned, the fellowship program hired various technical experts.

As I write this, globalization and the Internet with open-access courses and learning in every language have blown a massive hole in the secretive nature of who gets to know what. That access to knowledge, the rising costs of academic life, and advancements in judging on-the-job performance may place less value on academic learning and more value on workplace skills and competence. Though I'm proud of my doctorate and the effort it took to get it, I am glad to see these changes. As an experienced employer, I found that some degrees were necessary, but none were sufficient for people with weak interpersonal skills or poor emotional intelligence.

Understanding the differences among the three career paths and your preference is significant because of what happens in academic settings. If you are looking at graduate schools, there is a litmus test that will help you avoid what I have seen happen many times with early-career global health professionals. They wanted a career in implementation, but their graduate school taught them mainly research and paid little attention to the implementation skill set. As described in the Employers' Study, 85 percent of global health employers interviewed said that when it comes to nonclinical/health skills, academia can and should do better in preparing students for what the work is. That study and an examination of recent master's graduates in global health revealed that program management (i.e., implementation); program monitoring and evaluation; communications with clients, counterparts, and the community; strategy, project design, collaboration, and teamwork—as well as familiarity with the latest software—were significant weaknesses in professional preparation.

Be willing to take the business-of-one approach as early as graduate school selection. Review the core curricula from the lens of what employers value and your desired career. For example, if you'd like to be a project director implementing programs, don't attend a graduate program where most faculty are focused on research. If the stories they tell you are of long-distance relationships, gathering research data, and publishing, and they are less interested in how their findings are used, that might not be the school for you. If you want to be an excellent researcher and you've read and liked their research, then that school should be considered.

If despite these shortcomings a school still sounds attractive, consider what kind of workarounds you might create to tell a better story to future employers regarding your exposure and mastery of critical competencies. I now see students doing weekend workshops and certifications in project management. If allowed, they are taking courses in the business schools and the counseling programs that will enable them to be more competent coaches and managers. They are also seeking every opportunity to master software and technologies they see being used in the articles they read and the presentations they view on topics that matter to them. Some schools will not allow that flexibility, so check before you get stuck and create catchups or workarounds on the weekends.

If you are looking at graduate schools now or in the future, I suggest you assess the graduate program from your personal chief executive viewpoint and calculate that school's contribution to your career. Review what you can find out about the core faculty. Look at the faculty and the grants and side hustles they are involved in. Are they implementing programs in the field, or are they engaged in research studies? It matters if you sit under a technical expert for two to three years because their job is to teach you what they know. Just make sure they are preparing you for the career that you want.

Being a Great Student but a Poor Job Hunter

Sometimes, newly minted graduates with an advanced degree would come to me for an informational interview. Receiving an empathetic reception, they would pour out their frustration and shock at how foreign and challenging the job-hunting landscape is. They described a history of competence, success, and mastery as a student, sometimes throughout an MD or PhD program. Like Jennifer Macharia, described in the introduction to this book, this group feels at a loss in the job-hunting arena, experiencing failure and rejection for what sounded like the first time. This is another reason for academia to elevate career planning and work realities within their curricula, including making space for career-planning competencies as critical as the grades they get for their technical classes.

In the Employer's Study, global health employers talk about the in-service training they must provide to plug the holes left by academia. An astute career planner can predict and do that for themselves, putting them ahead of others competing for the same jobs.

I was lucky in that I had significant technical skills that Johns Hopkins desired, so they were willing to give me a solid education on the best practices of project implementation, including global health project design and implementation in the field, as well as anchoring in rigorous research, monitoring, and evaluation skills. I built my professional network on my own time and benefited greatly from USAID's Maximizing Access and Quality (MAQ) Working Groups, which brought me into close contact with professionals doing similar work. Still, graduate school is a great time to begin creating your professional network and connecting personally with faculty, colleagues, mentors, alums, and current students you find impressive or just like. Each new position builds your network; everyone needs tracking and reconnection over time. Those early relationships serve people twenty to forty years later as trusted participants in critical professional networks. I'll discuss such relationships in chapter 10 when we explore professional networking. Another recommendation is to subscribe to online job sites right away so you can begin tracking what kinds of jobs people are looking for. In other words, connect what you're learning to employment from the beginning. This may be a startling and profoundly new way of being a student. Not so for those who are doing midcareer changes and have started their graduate programs already focusing on a professional career strategy.

Midcareer and Senior Career Considerations

Special considerations exist for those who are already public health-related professionals who have worked domestically and are interested in working globally. This would include LMIC professionals who have had a career in their countries and want to move into the donor community, international NGOs, or any company doing business in international development, even if it is in their local town and the health system in which they have already worked. Others have worked for years in global health and are simply looking for a way to move forward. One of the reasons I emphasize the strategic nature of good career planning is that, once mastered, you can take these actions repeatedly even if the content, focus, and context change over time.

Other considerations that might not have been salient earlier in life begin to emerge during this period of professional growth. Issues related to family of origin can come to the fore. Aging parents may require your time and attention, calling you home. Sometimes, the location of children's educational needs becomes a priority, calling you to move closer to them. At other times, you or a family member might have health issues that limit your formerly global options, and one location becomes a priority. Given the higher potential for hybrid work, your location doesn't have to be a complete deal breaker, but it will be easier to negotiate if you are known and valued by your current/future employer.

The concept of being a business of one or the CEO of your own corporation is as salient in later career considerations as it is in early career. In fact, seasoned companies must be mindful of the surrounding environment if they are to remain viable. For example, when I met with LMIC fellows who had moved from their own countries' domestic work to what they considered global health work, I asked what they would advise others. Their standard advice included becoming aware of the business and career differences between the work setting and the industry, carefully reviewing job descriptions, and learning to reframe their current knowledge, skills, and experience using terms that were more reflective of rare, highly marketable global health skills and expertise.

Those who do not have health-related careers but see a place for themselves within the global health universe also need to follow their advice. Learn the language of global health, and do your due diligence to make the connection between your knowledge, skills, and experience and how they fit the needs of the organization you are attracted to. Don't know any organizations? Another task to add to your career-planning strategy. All this advice has been confirmed by people like you who have come before and by the findings in the Employers' Study, where global health employers reported they would hire someone with no overseas work experience if that person had a depth of sought-after expertise. Successful transitioners emphasized a career strategy that included Internet research, meeting attendance, and professional networking or developing a new, expanded professional network.

Many LMIC professionals with solid work experience in their own country want to work with a more significant multi-country focus or in the global health environment within their own country. Those who have been successful were technically competent and adept "culture mediators." They are true cross-cultural experts, having studied and learned the culture of the donor and having mastered effective communication, both in the official language and in nuance. Although the global forces of localization are calling for a new level of leadership and pushing back on the traditional roles and ways of doing business, I don't think the value of culture mediators will decrease.

As an LMIC professional, your cross-cultural expertise will not be questioned, though it should be, especially regarding your understanding of the donor culture and global health business. Most HIC professionals won't understand or consider the complexity of your culture with its own dynamic insider/outsider groupings and how this might help or hinder your ability to work in the field.

For an HIC professional, however, one of the biggest obstacles to a global career is the employers' expectations and value placed on overseas living and working experience. Substantial biases exist against HIC professionals who have not lived and worked overseas, especially in an LMIC country. The Employers' Study, the Recent Grad Study, and more recent publications confirm that bias, including the assumption that the experience makes you more cross-culturally competent. Academia has tried to ease the fact that most can't or won't offer that experience by setting up practicums and internships in local refugee communities and multicultural or low-income environments. Unfortunately, employers don't accept these experiences as valid sources of cross-cultural work experience (such as work done overseas). Even if you have those experiences, if you are from North America and obtain work in an international development organization, you will most likely be based in their US offices. The Recent Grad Study found that most recent MPH/MHS graduates wanted a job overseas, but the majority of them found work stateside. Working domestically is the most common way to begin working in global health.

I sometimes received calls from people who had applied for up to six fellowships and wanted to know if they should give up or keep applying.

I would tell them stories of global health professionals I knew who had applied multiple times, and then on that sixth or seventh application the fit was right, and they got the job. Being selected is a combination of the fit between you and the needs of the position and who else has applied for that position and their fit. You can't control these things, so don't beat yourself up. Let go of disappointment, and keep going. And if you need encouragement, use your professional and personal networks; if that doesn't work, call me.

Once you are actively looking, you will activate the rest of the steps in this book, including applying to positions that reflect your interests and skills, but remember that most get jobs via their professional network. It's never too late to review and update your professional network. See chapter 9 for more on this subject.

A special note to those who are senior career professionals. Even as you do your career strategic planning, senior staff have two special issues to consider. One is the responsibility you have for the next generation. Factor in some time and energy to give to those working through the problems you may have already figured out. Be a good guide, an active listener, and a generous reference. Also, be aware that significant international travel can affect health over time. Good food, exercise, sleep, and stress-management habits can keep your body from the toll of various diseases and chronic jet lag. At some point, one shifts from asking, "What do I want to be when I grow up? How can I be successful? How safe and secure can I be?" to "What will my legacy be?" Before jumping into retirement, consider planning a third act. Perhaps a new career or time focused on combining your gifts and your loves. I've noticed that with age comes more courage, less concern about what others think, and the development of a unique viewpoint that combines all my lessons and experiences. I still need to bring in income, but I'm more willing to risk doing only what I love and have expertise in. Creativity also has become a priority for me. We are all living longer, so whether you receive a salary or not, your third act is whatever you choose.

Making the Big Career Move: Domestic to/from Global, Jumping the Three Career Paths, and Changing Technical Areas

When I've coached people who wanted to make a significant change, however they defined it, it always starts with unsticking whatever definitions they have used to describe themselves previously. This is harder than one would think. In this process, they also redefine their marketable expertise, framing and labeling it in the new setting's environment. The next few chapters are going to help you sort through this process.

Consider writing down your responses to the questions below if you feel a significant change. I often use this sheet from WorkItDaily.com, adapted for this book. Consider this part of the work you might do to create your foundation (chap. 4) or to cultivate your vision (chap. 5). Or do it now for fun if you are thinking about making a significant career shift.

1. What about my current career don't I like?
2. What does this new career offer that my current career doesn't?
3. What are my core values, and how does this new career align with what is important to me?
4. What resources will I need to take advantage of these opportunities?
5. Do I know someone who is already in this career and can give me an honest insider's perspective?
6. Will my friends and family support this new career endeavor?
7. How long will living comfortably in this new career take?
8. Do I have the financial resources to make this new career work? If not, how can I get what I need to feel secure?
9. What are the long-term opportunities associated with this new career?
10. What struggles can I predict when transitioning to this new career?
11. What can I do now to minimize these potential struggles?

12. What specific experience do I hope to gain in this career move?
13. How will my previous experience help me in this new role?
14. Is this career move one step in a larger plan? If so, what does this new career need to provide to help me move forward?

One of my goals in this chapter was to reinforce that strategic career planning is essential in every working person's life and time. Different questions must be addressed throughout one's lifespan based on your situation during each period. Graduate school? What kind of graduate school? Overseas experience? What is the right career path for you at this moment? What's involved in the transition from one sector to another? Your business-of-one mentality will require you to take a strategic point of view throughout your life and not just at job-hunting time. Like good financial planning, checking in on yourself from that higher-level perspective and systematically tweaking your plans every so often (using my system, of course!) will ensure you avoid the full-blown panic and feeling of powerlessness that plagues so many who don't think about the big picture.

- PART II

BUILDING THE FOUNDATION

CHAPTER 4

Building the Foundation by Knowing Where You Are Now

- What's the best first step in my career-planning process?
- How do I use the four key questions to start building my career strategy?
- How can using mindfulness techniques, the awake inner observer, and self-reflection help me build the foundation for my career strategy?

Joseph Manchuria is a humble, highly competent communicator and public health professional who, if you ask, would tell you how self-observation and reflection contributed to his successful career (and life). You know him. He's one of those senior LMIC health professionals you want to work with because you trust and respect him. I first met Joseph at a conference where I was speaking. He was no longer an early-career physician working in his home country in eastern Africa. He took me aside during the conference for a chat about his career, and we eventually began to work together. Having worked his way up in the Ministry of Health, he also had a small private health clinic because federal wages were insufficient to support his family. So, he was doing direct service while working on public health policies in his technical areas. He was sought after by international donors to join HIC-funded projects in his country. As we worked together, he increased his "quiet time" after weekly church service, and then more frequently, he just sat in silence, repeating a favorite religious quote. He was used to asking God to hear his prayers but was working on improving the habit of being quiet, breathing deeply and slowly, with eyes shut, listening for God's answer. He described a developing perception that he could make a more significant difference by working for a larger international organization where he could potentially have a global impact. Retaining his humility but with confidence and courage, he developed a clear career road map, became more multiculturally savvy, and developed much better negotiating skills. He joined and has risen in a significant international organization where the difference he is making can be measured in millions of lives. You would probably know him if I said his real name. This fantastic outcome was supported by quiet moments and a stepwise career plan.

The first step to such professional success is an inquiry requiring self-reflection. Take advantage of this step if you are serious about building a flexible career planning strategy responsive to your ever-evolving life and focused on what is best for you. A good foundation will prevent you from making mistakes, selecting the wrong job, or staying in a career or position that doesn't support your best self.

When new clients come to me, they often have a particular issue in mind, such as finding out more about global health careers, updating their résumés, or preparing for an interview. They have a general sense of being stuck and wanting more movement in their careers. Sometimes they are senior professionals who want to take their careers to the next level. Occasionally, my clients describe themselves as depressed, wrestling with newly experienced failures in job hunting despite a history of academic success. Jokes they once made about the imposter syndrome are no longer funny. Besides the clients described in the introduction who had similar issues, there was another client, whom we've called Heather Brown, an American who recently received a master's degree in public health. Her whole life has been spent mastering academia, and she has done a spectacular job—high grade-point average, beloved and respected by her teachers. She came to me because she wanted help developing a career plan. She had no substantial professional network, but it was a good start. She was articulate, intelligent, and ambitious but tended to insecurity. It took a few sessions, but slowly, she shared the secret she had been harboring—that she's not as great as the compliments she receives. She knows that someday, someone will discover this truth, and she will be let go, run out, or maybe she will never get that tremendous postgraduate job. Everyone seems so much better than her. Heather is ambitious but secretly lacks self-confidence. Since she had previously done so exceptionally well, she was now confused by how "stuck" she felt in her career planning and how often she felt stressed, moving toward depression. This double dynamic had left her frightened and frozen. She knew how to be a student but started feeling unsure she would do well in a professional environment. It was critical to uncover and help her articulate her just-below-awareness thoughts. I used simple cognitive behavioral techniques (more on this in chap. 6) to help separate the facts of her situation and get clear about the meaning her mind had attached to those thoughts, which resulted in the feelings, the actions, and the results she was getting. Once she understood this process and intentionally practiced choosing different thoughts, it was much easier for her to take control over her career planning, using the tools and process as successfully as she had mastered being a student.

Another example is what I have learned from those LMIC health professionals who have concluded that foreign donor–resourced health work pays better and can be more empowering. They want information on bridging the gap between where they are now and where they would like to go professionally. Recently, a client shared with me an Excel spreadsheet of a complete career plan, but it contained zero deviations or space for surprises and twists, like pandemics! There is often a tremendous amount of anxiety and concern but also an impatience to take time for the most critical step—laying the foundation.

I will help them with their most immediate needs, often focused on résumés and interviews. They hired me, and I owe them that immediate sense of moving forward. But I also want to help them create a set of career-planning habits that can be used for the rest of their professional lives. My experience is that those who do that also check in with me occasionally as a trusted lifetime advisor. A career strategy foundation should accommodate all the twists and turns of life's surprises and serve you no matter where life takes you. The one thing I know for sure is that things will go differently than expected. Situations will arise that an updated résumé or an excellent LinkedIn account will not address. One takeaway from this book is the critical importance of an awake inner observer running your business and framing your life needs to be as essential to your career-planning agenda.

I've worked with many clients for whom self-reflection is challenging to experience. It may seem like a luxury or a "Western" thing. But research on the human brain has confirmed this state is part of our biology. Multiple studies have also reinforced the power of these short periods (sometimes five to ten minutes daily is all you need) for various health and happiness benefits. For our purposes, these moments of reflection open us to more profound answers to essential questions. I'm proposing an inquiry, a simple set of four questions that will guide you in collecting information critical to making informed decisions about the career you sometimes don't even know you want or could have. Understanding how you think and where you are in these four areas will prevent you from taking positions and deciding on career paths that do not feed your soul or your bank account or make strategic sense for your unique story.

Self-reflection can help cut through our brain's noise and self-talk. Every person's brain is talking to them all the time, right? For our purposes, self-reflection is an inquiry—a simple set of four questions that will guide you in collecting information critical to making informed decisions about the best professional environment and career for you right now. The inner observer represents your most profound truth. It is the voice of your true self. It is awakened in many ways and can take many forms. I'm going to mention mindfulness and meditation because they are so accessible.

Mindfulness is a foundational activity for awakening your inner observer. According to John Kabat Zin, mindfulness is intentionally paying attention to the present moment, without judgment. There are a thousand ways to foster a quiet mind and a compassionate heart, another prerequisite for bone-deep success. Some of those ways include formal meditation and informal practices such as intentionally using the breath to foster a quiet mind while walking, swimming, doing Tai Chi or yoga, cleaning, driving, gardening, eating, showering, serving your family or the community, and so on. You get the point—you can choose many approaches to mindfulness. Plenty of science shows that regular and intentional mindfulness practice changes the brain. A long list of positive health and emotional changes resulting from practices that are as short as ten minutes. This is also reflected in my real-world experience with a practice I started in 1971 and fostered off and on until the 1990s, when it became a consistent morning practice. I know those with solid self-reflection and mindfulness practices do very well in Step 1, even surprising themselves with new ideas that just come to them in the listening space.

Let's take a moment to discuss getting to know your inner observer. Who is that neutral observer, and how do you awaken the impartial, objective, yet loving voice? One calm, quiet moment at a time. It is that part of you that some of us experience as the cheerleading captain of our fan club, especially if we have a history of only hearing negative and critical self-talk. That loving voice is the reflection of your true self. Recently, I was on a panel at an academic conference with my editor on the experience of moving from publishing journal articles to writing books. In the audience was a senior, brilliant, well-regarded global health expert who has received rewards and accolades for his many achievements. During the question-and-answer segment and later in a private conversation, he expressed his heart's desire to write a book, but his internal dialogue was telling him he had nothing to say. Having been a fan of his for years, it broke my heart to hear him perfectly describe the need to awaken the inner observer and start addressing habitual thoughts that no longer serve him.

The awake inner observer, the voice I've been describing, loves you, supports you, wants the best for you, and reflects an inner, deeper knowing. In my cosmology, we are not broken but perfect and worthy of all good things. So many of us go through our lives as though we are sleepwalking, with little self-reflection. Our hectic minds enslave us with much chatter, and that chatter is often our inner critic telling us all the ways that we are making mistakes and doing things wrong, sometimes with a dose of shame. It's this inner drumbeat of "I am not enough," "I am not worthy," "I am not good enough." It is human nature to spend most of our conscious time focusing on the past or planning the future. That chatter is how your brain tries to protect you and make things safe. This topic will surface again in Step 3, when we discuss the attitude adjustment necessary to address the distorted thoughts that paralyze us.

How often can you visit the space where you have a deep sense of being ok with everything? Mother Teresa described this to me as we debated family planning in an isolated African hotel. I was a team member helping government experts design a new multiyear adolescent health strategy. Mother Teresa was in the country expanding her order, which created orphanages to give young girls another kind of choice post-pregnancy and care for every abandoned infant. A devoted Catholic, she did not believe adolescents should have any information or access to modern family planning methods. She joined our group, and throughout our time together—with the electricity going off and on, with no hot water ever—we went head to head. Why? Because I was an advocate for information and access based on the mountain of research I'd learned during my time at Johns Hopkins University. But in the dusty, humid, mosquito-ridden room, sitting at a rickety wooden table over many cups of tea, my time with Mother Teresa also forced me to get quiet and dig deep into my heart so that my opinions were much more anchored and consistent with my awake inner observer and loving toward those who disagreed with me. Because being a Roman Catholic was my first religious identity, I quaked before this extremely short, deeply holy, opinionated woman. In the end, the national strategy included information and access for those young people, including the girls who often died from having babies too young, too many, and too close together. But I'll never forget how Mother Teresa forced me to test my opinions, not just with data but with deep reflection on why I think and feel the way I do.

Do you want to activate that inner observer? Do you want to awaken and make that space more accessible? I'm being sneaky here because awakening our inner observer has many benefits beyond developing a supportive, authentic career planning strategy.

The foundation is laid when you can answer your questions to your satisfaction. Your answers to the four questions listed below will change over time, and I recommend an annual check-in with yourself. If you are religious, you can label that awake inner observer in any way that makes sense and feels comfortable. For me, it is the voice of my true and best self. My true self accepts me and loves me exactly as I am and never tells me I'm a total fraud, should be ashamed of myself, or other negative thoughts. The imposter syndrome resides in that part of the brain, which we will deal with later.

Why all this fuss about the awake inner observer, mindfulness, and all that? Because the foundation for a lifetime, always-relevant career strategy starts with your capacity to know where you are now in a profound way. I recommend that you write down your answers. The physical act of writing can help you think more creatively and generate ideas more freely. It also allows you to focus and concentrate. When you write by hand, you are less likely to be distracted by the many notifications and distractions that come with using a computer. Writing by hand also allows for greater personalization and customization. Further, research has shown that it helps with memory retention and recall. You want these ideas readily available to you as you design your strategy. Your priority is to create detailed answers to the following four questions.

1. What do I love to do?

Nobody likes everything they are doing all the time in their jobs or their lives. It is expected to have parts of your work that you don't care for or make you more anxious, bored, or stressed. You supply the word that represents the worst parts of your job. Often, this has to do with your personal preferences (being alone versus with others), the characteristics of the people you work with (kind/cruel, smart/dumb), specific tasks (creative or mundane), the volume of activity, pace, and more. All people and jobs are neutral. It's the meaning that you attach to it that makes these answers important.

Commit to this simple process: take a moment two to four times a day (you can set reminders on your cellphone if you like), and ask yourself, "Do I love what I'm doing right now?" Trust that your inner observer will supply you with an answer. Watch yourself as you are doing whatever it is. You want to build opinions and self-knowledge about your preferences. Think of yourself as a scientist gathering data on your professional life. You don't have to rush to interpretation, analysis, results, and recommendations. Be open to deepening understanding as you go through the layers. You're just collecting information. When you're in that moment, and you know something is happening that is bringing you joy, what is it? What is happening when some deep need is being met? When all seems right with the world? As the organizational guru Marie Kondo would say, it's about what sparks joy. Please take note of that because it is essential in your analysis process. You may have just a few items, or you may have many things. If you have zero items that spark joy, acknowledge that you're in a difficult situation but you still want to learn from that situation, and there will be activities or actions or states that feel better than others. Sort those out and write them down.

Now is the time to notice the difference between your inner critic and observer. Which one has the stronger voice? Who is taking up residence in your brain? This inquiry is a great tool to awaken or strengthen the inner observer and put some boundaries around the inner critic, which, when left unchallenged, will make your life miserable.

2. What am I good at?

The response to this second question follows the same process: you call upon that part of you that is your awakened inner observer. You are alerting a part of your brain by setting an intention in the morning that you will receive answers to the question, "What am I good at?" or "What are my gifts?" Be aware that what you're good at may differ from what you love. There might be overlap, but there might not. It's not just what you think but also what kind of feedback you receive from others. When you receive praise from others or compliments over the day, a week, a month, or a year, what are they saying about you? When you feel a moment of pride, is it a simple interaction, a deadline met, some solid writing (yes, emails count), a successful meeting you facilitated, or some other significant contribution? Discipline yourself to tune into all the things that go right in a week because you will be fighting against the brain's negative bias, one of those leftovers from cave person days.

When I first started in global health, I did a consultancy in Kenya. The director of the Family Planning Association of Kenya sent to my employer, Johns Hopkins University, a letter praising and thanking them for sending me, describing how helpful I was. I put the letter in my "happy file," the contents of which still lift me. (I'll have more to say on the happy file concept in chap. 7.) These laudatory remarks had a significant effect on how those in authority perceived me but also on how I saw myself. I realized that even though there was so much I didn't know about global health, I had the basic chops regarding critical competencies. I examined what I had done that they liked and just did more of that. For example, I often get highly rated on my organizational development activities. Yet these are not my "first love" activities. The one-on-one conversations matter most to me, so my career now focuses on being a lifetime trusted advisor to individuals rather than facilitating team building.

3. Where do I want to be geographically?

The third inquiry is noticing and collecting information about your current situation. Imagine yourself in a particular city or country. Create a small list of serious possibilities. They can be specific or general, but they should be possibilities in that they have potential for professional advancement. And then think about where you are now. What are the upsides and downsides of each of those possibilities? The aspects of your current life that make these possibilities attractive (or not) will begin to emerge. For example, are you starting a global health career without working or living overseas? The Employers' Study indicates that global health employers will say they are happy to hire those with domestic experience only. Still, they tend only to do that if you have deep technical depth in an area they need, which favors the more experienced professional. I remember doing an informational interview with a brand-new PhD in global health who eventually tearfully shared her deep fear and frustration over her unsuccessful job hunt. She was too educated to take an entry-level role. Still, she had never lived or worked overseas or developed management skills, so her experience was considered insufficient for the more senior roles, which typically presume significant work experience in LMIC environments and running teams. Why didn't her academic program do a better job of helping her prepare for what would be needed in the work? I will never forget her difficult situation, which could have been alleviated with academia's better planning and more understanding of, or caring about, what students' lives would be like postgraduation. Because you now know this, you can plan to ensure you are not left to burrow out of this professional hole. By the way, she figured out her experience gaps, took an academic position, and created a strategy to eventually move into the work she wanted to do. I wish her well.

Besides the professional strategies related to overseas living and working experience, another factor that often influences one's geographic preferences is lifespan, or stage in life. Many want to be close to their parents as they age. Many want to be close to their children if they are attending college in their home country. Some like to ensure that as they progress in their careers, they can eventually return to their own countries and make a difference. Sometimes, they yearn for the comfort of one's own culture. Occasionally, one's partner is the person who is tired of living where you are now and either wants to go home or move to another culture or that is necessary for their career progression.

There can be a cost to being bicultural. My mother, an Australian, met my American naval officer dad during World War II at a USO dance in Melbourne, her hometown. They married, and she moved to the United States with my older brother and lived there. After becoming a widow, she returned often to Australia. She described the yearning she felt to be with her American children in the United States while longing for the comfort of being in her own culture. She never felt completely comfortable in either space, always missing one country. I felt compassion for her. I share this story because there can be a cost to being bicultural and savvy; sensitive professionals consider the potential costs and benefits of all options. LMIC professionals who have spent years raising their children in a HIC environment, noticing who their children are becoming, may know what I'm talking about.

The third question will prompt answers that change over time and are affected by significant trends and their profound effects on work life and global health business. The COVID-19 pandemic has led to the normalization of virtual workspaces. As of 2021, the best human resources research tells us that it is doubtful that we will return to the in-person workspace as the only option. As we figure this out over time, we will gain a balance between the power of the in-person connection and technological advances that facilitate connection at the virtual level. Also, as climate change makes some geographies more livable than others, a virtual or hybrid environment with some in-person and some virtual work is likely to become more common. Besides AI, technology will evolve the work-life options in ways I cannot predict, significantly influencing the questions and opportunities you will consider when responding to this question.

4. What skills and knowledge will organizations pay for?

Answering this question requires a slightly different approach than the previous inquiries because it takes some research before you can analyze the data you have collected. Your research should include (1) finding out what the global health trends are from the perspective of KASE—what knowledge, attitudes, skills, and experience are reflected in those trends—and (2) what positions are paying by reviewing current vacancies attractive to you and their salaries, as well as what people in your professional network know about salary ranges in various organizations.

To track global health trends, identify the best groups presenting the most exciting data and analysis closest to your career interests. Several reputable websites provide big-picture global health data and are frequently cited by researchers, policymakers, and the public:

- World Health Organization (www.who.int). As you probably know, WHO is a specialized agency of the United Nations responsible for global public health. Its website provides comprehensive information on global health issues, including disease outbreaks, health systems, and health equity.
- Institute for Health Metrics and Evaluation (www.healthdata .org). The IHME is an independent global health research organization at the University of Washington. It provides comprehensive data on global health trends, including disease burden, risk factors, and health financing.
- Global Burden of Disease Study (http://www.thelancet.com/ gbd). This is my favorite website when the GBD study comes out, though it will also appear on other websites, including IHME. The GBD is a collaborative effort between the IHME and the WHO that estimates the global disease and injury burden. I particularly like how the website includes interactive data visualizations, detailed reports, and publications.
- Centers for Disease Control and Prevention (www.cdc.gov). The CDC is a US federal agency responsible for protecting public health and safety. Its website provides data and information on global health threats, including infectious diseases, chronic diseases, and environmental health hazards.

These are just a few examples of the most frequently cited websites for big-picture global health worldwide data. Many other organizations and resources provide valuable information on global health issues, and researchers should carefully assess the reliability and validity of any data they use. There are also frequent webinars, probably in your specific technical area, that can supply you with predictions regarding the future. You just need to examine the data from a career perspective. Understanding trends in global health may help you uncover new areas of interest and help you predict what skills and knowledge will be helpful (and marketable) in the future. Keep building on this list yourself, particularly related to your specific interests.

Global trends in health, especially unmet needs, significant suffering, and the giant killers, all can provide data on where governments and donors might be leaning toward investing in the future and the kind of knowledge and skill sets that will be most in demand. This is particularly true of the first competency cluster, health expertise (described in chap. 2), which focuses on technical health topics and specific populations. Be aware, however, that what kills the most people is not always where donors make their most significant investments. There are many reasons for that, including the priority of health security, so you will also need to use additional data points, such as patterns of job postings in the most common GH job-hunting websites and your professional network, to provide valuable data for you to analyze. Some popular websites list global health career vacancies (Appendix B contains a list of these). Create your own list of those positions that are closest to your desired work. It is an excellent opportunity to strengthen your tracking skills and select your favorite resources. Many organizations are starting to advertise salary ranges, giving you valuable data about the going rates of different levels of experience and expertise. But don't forget to consider and anticipate future trends. If you are only chasing the current funding, you will always be behind.

You also want to identify organizations that are interesting to you for potential employment, and track their websites and activities to discover what they say about themselves and their priorities. Of course, the websites are typically run by communication, public relations, and image departments, so you may have to dig deep to discover their values and the feel of working there.

Besides Internet sources, your professional network is a handy, typically untapped resource. It's so important that I wrote chapter 9 with a focus on designing, developing, and caring for professional networks. Talk with people, and instead of asking them what their salaries are, ask them what they think someone would pay for the work and experience that reflects your vision of your future work. Building an expanded professional network and conducting your own research are particularly important when considering a career change.

This is also an excellent opportunity to develop your knowledge management and tracking skills by developing your favorite resources. Answering question 4 helps keep you tuned into the bigger picture of global health and employment trends. I explored knowledge management skills in chapter 3, but for now, identify and use your favorite Internet sources and your sources of intel about what's going on. Efficiently focusing on global health trends will factor into your status assessment and give you valuable information to consider the market for your business of one.

Savvy career strategists—like you—consider all this information in their own personal "state of the union." Seasoned by your own experience, you use the collected and analyzed data to create an explicit and informed image of what you love about work, your gifts, preferred locations, where the industry is going, what is currently valued, and how it is weighted. In chapter 5, you will create a clearer picture of the future you envision. The more informed you are about the global health microstate and career implications, the more likely you are to engage in honest conversations where you are co-creating a future relationship with your prospective employer.

CHAPTER 5

Creating the Vision

- Why is creating a vision of my future professional self so important?

- How do I create a clear picture of myself in the global health professional life I want?

After you have a solid analysis of where you are now, it's time to get clear about the future you want to move toward. Remember Heather Brown from the book's introduction? She was an American who had recently received a master's degree in public health. Her whole life had been focused on successfully mastering the academic student identity. Now that she was seeking what she considered her first professional position, she had become frozen by memories of past humiliations, was fearful of rejection, and was experiencing the real pain that comes from feeling unworthy. She was both ambitious and self-doubting. She hid both exceptionally well and was confused by how "stuck" she felt in her career planning and how much stress she was experiencing.

Many famous writers and motivational speakers have written about developing a personal vision. Stephen Covey is known for his book *The 7 Habits of Highly Effective People*, which discusses the importance of individual vision and setting clear life goals. Tony Robbins is a well-known motivational speaker and author who has written books like *Awaken the Giant Within*, which explores creating a compelling personal vision. In books like *The Monk Who Sold His Ferrari*, Robin Sharma discusses the idea of making a personal vision and living a fulfilling life. Finally, my guide for the past decade has been Eckhart Tolle, whose *The Power of Now* focuses on living in the present moment and finding clarity in your life's purpose.

From different perspectives, various experts support the effectiveness of creating a vision of our future and then supporting that vision with a series of incremental goals. In chapter 6, we'll talk more about setting goals, but I'd like to introduce several vital concepts now. One of my favorite productivity experts, Lindsay Satterfield, says that goals affect your actions. Those who develop and use goals report experiencing more confidence, achievement, success, and fulfillment. Bringing a vision into existence requires conscious thought, intention, and belief. It involves aligning your mindset, emotions, and actions with your wish to attract or achieve what you desire. I am not claiming a science-based manifestation process, but there are psychological and cognitive processes that can explain how our vision and goals can be achieved. Taking my cues from the work of John Locke, Stephen Covey, and Carolyn S. Dweck (see the Further Reading section), below are some necessary factors.

1. Clarifying vision and intentions. The first step in manifesting a vision is clearly defining your ultimate desire and intentions. This involves visualizing what you want to achieve, setting specific and measurable goals, and being aware of your desires.

2. Positive thinking and mindset. Maintaining a positive mindset can help you achieve your vision. Positive thinking can influence your attitude, motivation, and perseverance. It can also enhance your problem-solving abilities and help you focus.

3. Visualization and mental imagery. Visualization is a technique where you mentally imagine yourself achieving your desired outcome. By vividly picturing your goals, you engage your brain's visual and emotional centers, which can reinforce your motivation and increase your belief in the possibility of success.

4. Belief and self-efficacy. Believing in yourself and your ability to achieve your goals is crucial. Heather, despite observable evidence to the contrary, struggled with this factor the most. Building self-efficacy involves developing confidence in your skills and capabilities. Research suggests that individuals with high self-efficacy are more likely to act and persist in facing challenges. In chapter 6, we'll explore some techniques to help you manage how we talk ourselves out of success and how we can fix that.

5. Action and effort. Manifesting a vision requires acting and making consistent efforts toward your goals. While positive thinking and visualization are valuable, they must be accompanied by concrete steps and work. Action is often the catalyst that turns vision into reality. Although each chapter in this book describes actions for you to take, the concluding chapters are mainly focused on implementable action steps.

6. Focus and attention. Focusing on your vision can help you align your thoughts, emotions, and actions with your desired outcome. You can filter out distractions and stay committed to necessary career-related tasks and activities by directing your attention toward your goals. You may feel shy or reticent about being invited to focus on developing a vision. Heather's secret sense of unworthiness increased her reticence, conflicting with her tremendous energy and desire to make a difference. Visioning isn't just about the job you want but the life you want. Your vision may not include any aspect of "standing out" but may be focused on "doing good" or "finding peace." A vision is valuable if it is connected to your deepest desires.

7. Creating a vision provides a crucial focal point and strengthens your capacity to see or project into the future. This focus helps you make decisions—this and not that—so you are more likely to move forward. Now is the time to get specific and granular.

Heather felt compelled by the desire to help decrease infant mortality, but it wasn't showing up in any of her job-hunting materials. In her visioning work, she struggled with a sense that if she "chose" one vision, it would preclude her from other possibilities and paths. I assured her that visioning is a vital organizing tool in professional development, but it is not static. Visions shift as new data come in and require refinement or adjustment. Sometimes visions blur and need refocusing. These are lifetime career strategies, not a task done once and for all.

When I see people rolling their eyes as we start talking about visioning, I understand that they see this as impractical and unnecessary. But people who are successful in achieving goals can see the outlines of the endgame. They can project themselves into an unknown future. This is the creative power that we all have, and it is the genesis of every vision. So, in this part of the process, we project ourselves into the future and look around. It is brainstorming without censoring, editing, qualifying, judging, or filtering. Write down whatever comes to mind, even if it seems wacky or out there. You can share your thoughts with others whom you trust—or not. Let your imagination run wild, and create a picture of yourself living the life you want.

The mind has a natural generative capacity. It's an idea machine, so before you narrow the field and select your goals, it's essential to let the mind roam free and generate ideas and possibilities from which to choose. So, start with where you'd like to be three to five years from now. I generally advise starting with a three- to five-year vision and then reenvisioning check-ins with trusted others as a part of your career strategy. This allows you to consider information that has shifted since your last effort. I no longer suggest ten-year goals because we work increasingly in a VUCA environment where volatility, uncertainty, complexity, and ambiguity reign. Visioning is the bold act of a creator. Innovation, change, and achievement all start with seeing what's needed, what's missing, what's hoped for, what it's time for, what's called for, what's inspiring, what's possible, or what's desired.

Project yourself into the future. What do you see? What is your life like? How do you feel? What are you doing? What's different from now?

What's the same? What's your day like? What's your lifestyle like? What are you proud of? What have you accomplished or contributed to it? Your dream doesn't have to make sense. Let yourself dream and write down what you see, brainstorm-style. What does success look like? What is soul-satisfying work? What is the compensation you need to feel successful or comfortable? Where are you located? Are you figuring in a partner? Children? Family? In this judgment-free moment, what matters to you?

Heather was typical in that the conversation and the writing were general, and then she began to review her thinking, writing a more detailed picture. The result was that she watched a mother hold her infant son receiving a food supplement. The mother then measured her son with a measure-at-home tape, with the mother smiling that her baby boy was out of danger and doing much better. Another aspect of her vision included her at a prestigious conference, making a presentation on her publication about the infant nutrition program she had co-led with an LMIC partner, leading to incredible results. Her husband and her child were in the audience at the presentation. And she herself looked healthy and fabulous! Notice that this vision included aspects of her heart's desire with no assumption of controlling all the circumstances of success.

Now that you've brainstormed possible futures, look back at what you wrote. What do you notice about your list? What surprises you and why? What makes you nervous and why? What excites you and why? What seems impossible and why? What themes do you notice? What's missing? Keep tailoring it until the picture you have painted is in full color.

You now have a vision statement, a set of goals sorted by three-month segments, and comments regarding why those goals are important to you. Before we turn the goals into actions and milestones for the next three months, we must examine the differences between where you are now (discussed in chap. 4) and where you want to go (discussed in this chapter). In chapter 6, we'll do a gap analysis, which will influence the next step in our process: the development of a set of actions and milestones that you might take within the next three months that would result in reaching your three-month goals.

CHAPTER 6

Identifying the Gaps

- What steps can I use to analyze all the information I've collected to identify critical, bridgeable gaps between where I am now and where I want to go?

- How do I uncover the gaps in my knowledge, attitudes, skills, and experience that get in the way of my vision for my professional life?

- How can I identify outdated thoughts, ensuring my thinking supports my goals rather than limits them and ultimately my success?

When exploring competencies in chapter 2, I referenced KASE: knowledge, attitudes, skills, and experience. This chapter focuses on what knowledge, behavioral skills, experiences, and attitudes you need to identify and address to bridge the gap and move into your desired future. We will spend some time dissecting the distorted, outdated thinking that keeps you from setting and achieving the goals leading to your best future. I have found that this is one of the most significant barriers to professionals moving forward. From an employment viewpoint, I include experience because it is such a critical part of the story from an employer's point of view. Employers use "experience" as a shorthand to assume you have the needed knowledge, attitudes, and skills. This step is crucial for career changers who must interpret their knowledge, attitudes, skills, and experience in the context and language relevant to global health employers. Don't expect employers to do this work. It's up to you, and you can do it!

There are trends and common issues in global health, no matter what country you call home, but your status and vision are unique. Only some KASE items will be relevant to you personally. This chapter is to get you started in your planning. At this stage in your process, you probably have your writings from chapters 4 and 5, which you can now reference as you actively work to identify and address any gaps that may keep you out of the running for the work you want to do and the life you want to lead. Your vision is what narrows down this work to only what serves you in progressing down your unique path.

Step 1 is to analyze your knowledge, skills, and experience via competencies. In chapter 2, you read about big-picture competency trends. Now that you have a clear sense of your desired future, look at those areas again and imagine yourself in a job interview, speaking confidently about what you know and can do. Imagine yourself on the job in that beautiful mental space of trusting your expertise but being excited about your capacity to be creative and learn even more. That has always been my sweet spot—I know what I'm doing, but I'm also stretching myself in new ways. If new experiences or learning are required, you'll address that later in this chapter on goal setting. Your measuring stick for identifying your gaps is your vision. Consider what gaps you need to address to increase your marketability over time. If you haven't done it yet, now is the time to examine your knowledge, skills, and experience in the areas described in chapter 2:

  I. Health Expertise
 II. The Business of Global Health
III. Intrapersonal and Interpersonal Effectiveness
 IV. Technology and Knowledge Management

Review your own experience and rate yourself from these choices on a Likert scale from 1 to 5:

1. awareness, observer, or neophyte
2. acquiring, learner, or novice
3. developing, contributor, or apprentice
4. intermediate, practitioner, or journeyman
5. advanced, expert, or guru

Step 2 is to review your answers to the four key questions in chapter 4, where you added more context and big-picture thinking to your career strategy. Take the work you did in chapter 4 (or do it now) when you thoroughly examined your current professional status and reviewed what is out there in the fourth question. A well-researched response to question 4 means you also have essential data regarding knowledge, skills, or experience gaps.

In step 3, you are reviewing the visioning work that you did in chapter 5. All the work you've done now gets compared against the professional life in your vision, and this is when your most critical gaps are identified. You are taking the considerable information you have gathered regarding the global health profession and making a list of the gaps you want to start working on.

Step 4 is to take all the data you've collected thus far and add in the employer's perspective. You may have already done some of this work when responding to question 4 in chapter 4. Reviewing global health job websites is an excellent way to compare what you bring and the current job market needs. I list the most popular global health websites for job hunters in Appendix B. See my website (https://www .drsharonrudy.com) for any updates.

This chapter benefits career strategists who can analyze their KASE against an employer's expectations and interpret their experience to satisfy the hiring staff. When perusing employment websites, look for at least five job descriptions most fitting your vision. Now, check the qualifications:

Where is the workplace located (virtual, in-office, hybrid)?
How many years of experience are required?
Which degrees are preferred?
What are the experiences they expect you to have?
Do you need overseas *working* experience? Or is just *living* experience enough?
What languages do they expect you to be able to work in?
What do they expect you to know?
What do they expect you to be able to do?
What can you glean from the soft skills description they might have included?

Common considerations from a review of jobs, your current résumé, and your vision are the need to develop technical global health knowledge, skills that make you more attractive as an employee, and experiences such as supervision, management, and cross-cultural expertise. For HIC professionals, the experience of working and living overseas has proven to be an essential criterion for differentiating résumés, so if you lack such experience and most job postings require it, consider making a move abroad a priority. It may mean relocating to a preferred country without a position, because obtaining one or negotiating for a stateside position with a field focus is often easier. This is only for the brave. If early career, consider organizations, like the Peace Corps, that will send you overseas.

For LMIC professionals who aspire to more success in the currently HIC-dominated donor and implementer communities, consider the knowledge and skills related to the business of global health. Look at those from your continent who have successfully transitioned into positions you might be interested in. One standard skill set is the ability to be a culture mediator. Both in language and demeanor, successful GH professionals connect across cultures in ways that make everyone comfortable. Consider taking charge of the narrative, moving from a goal of being a valued consultant or an employee of a major international organization to envisioning yourself as someone successfully competing against an HIC nonprofit, for-profit, or academic organization for the contract—and winning! Insist on being treated with respect and fighting the colonial mentality with new boundaries and expectations. See chapter 2 for more information regarding locally-led development, and observe those who have come before you.

Step 5: When I described the critical competency of interpersonal skills, it was based on everything I've learned as a practitioner, an employer, and now as a coach and lifetime advisor. This is the "attitude" aspect of KASE. Because it is such a critically important key to success, I've focused on using cognitive behavioral techniques as a simple way to self-analyze and self-coach. I'm using the identification of distorted thinking as an accessible pathway to these powerful, subtle habits of thought that can become obstacles to our goals.

From your review of position descriptions and the lists of knowledge, skills, and experiences you are analyzing, you will develop a list of things you should know and have had successful experiences to set you up. Plugging those gaps is critical, but you will face frustrating obstacles if you don't address your attitude. It's your feelings, emotions, and how your thoughts keep you from the future you want. We are going to explore that next.

Many global health researchers and evaluators in behavior change will relate to KAP (knowledge, attitudes, and practice) or KAB (knowledge, attitude, and behavior) when measuring change in targeted populations. These are often used as measures of change in a defined population regarding health—did the person increase their knowledge, change their feelings about or attitude toward something, or has the behavior changed in some manner? We can apply these measures to ourselves as well. Previously, we've been exploring the experience and knowledge that shows up in professional behavior. Now it's time to think about attitudes or, at their core, emotions or feelings. I'm using "attitudes" to encompass our feelings and unexamined, below-conscious thoughts that result in those feelings. This concept is critical to successfully reaching the life you want because unexamined thoughts will limit your choices, options, planning, vision, and ultimately what happens in your life.

There are two essential activities where the information you have collected from the inquiry gets analyzed and becomes actionable. The first is identifying gaps in knowledge, skills, and experience, which we have just explored. The second is uncovering thought distortions. What would be helpful in this activity is another person—perhaps a mentor, coach, or someone who knows you well professionally and whom you trust—or the act of writing your thoughts down, then coming back another day to review them with fresh eyes. While you are asking, developing, and sharing answers to your four key questions; exploring your current situation; and creating your vision, another part of you or someone else is listening for those two actionable topics: missing knowledge/skills/experience and limiting beliefs.

It is tough to be the thinker of your thoughts and the observer simultaneously. A strengthened inner observer knows the difference between your thoughts and the factual reality of a situation. Like most people, I learned what to think from my parents, teachers, other essential role models, and external sources. I watched and took in all the messages about myself, others, and the world. I took in all these lessons to make sense of the world around me. I also built strategies to survive and sometimes thrive in my growing-up years. This is what we all do. The challenge is that with our child-size abilities and young brains, we occasionally take in distorted, negative thinking that generates enormous suffering. If we become parents, we can pass this suffering on to our children. Sometimes, distorted thinking combines with our biology to create such suffering that we choose destructive coping mechanisms; occasionally, we do not survive our thinking. That's how severe and damaging thought distortions can be.

Our worst failure is no more than a mental construct and can teach us to live through and process the feelings we are most afraid of. I spent some time in Tanzania, supporting women in Africa who had been victims of unthinkable rape and torture, sometimes by former friends and neighbors during the Rwandan genocide. No matter what their injuries and trauma, which were profound, I noticed there was a variation in the meanings they attached to these events as well as their ability to process and live through the most horrible emotional and physical injuries. These variations significantly affected their ability to survive and even thrive regardless of the unimaginable things in their lives. I was reminded of the two years I spent volunteering at the Gainesville Suicide and Crisis Prevention Center in the 1970s during my first graduate school experience. I supported victims of rape and other violent crimes, and I recall one of them patiently explaining to me that she was refusing to allow thirty minutes of trauma to dictate the rest of her life. Her journey back to wholeness was not easy, but she could call back and empower herself. She, like some of the Rwandan women, was choosing to process her thoughts in a way I had never seen before, and I learned a lot from all of them. The processing of our thoughts—choosing those that serve us rather than diminish us—can help us in every aspect of our lives.

I know this sounds heavy, but thought distortions also significantly limit your thinking in career planning. They limit your choices, the options you're willing to consider, and your abilities to reach beyond what you think is possible. When we live in fear, courage becomes an unfamiliar theoretical condition. Yet it is available to each of us, and learning to sit through the discomfort is a critical component of a deeply satisfying and fulfilling professional life.

I was trained early on as a cognitive behaviorist in my first graduate program. Still, it is only in the past few years that I integrated a five-factor model into my work that allows us to coach ourselves. It is based on cognitive behavioral therapy (CBT) techniques adopted by Brooke Castillo, who founded the Life Coaching School. CBT emerged in the 1950s and 1960s as a form of psychotherapy. It emphasizes the role of thoughts and beliefs in shaping behavior and emotions. It is rooted in the idea that maladaptive thinking and behavior patterns can be changed by developing new, more adaptive ways of thinking and behaving. Other pioneers in the genre include Albert Bandura, whose work focused on social learning theory and self-efficacy; Aaron Beck; and Albert Ellis, who called it rational emotive behavior therapy (REBT). CBT practitioners work to enhance self-efficacy by helping individuals develop more adaptive ways of thinking and problem solving.

Bandura's contributions to CBT also include the concept of self-regulation. Self-regulation refers to an individual's ability to monitor and control their behavior, thoughts, and emotions. Coaches use the model, but it is also a self-help tool based on the idea that many of us need help to strengthen self-regulation skills, such as identifying and challenging negative thoughts and implementing coping strategies, to manage our thinking more effectively.

Our brain is not always our best friend, so we must learn to think about and observe our thoughts with conscious awareness. Yet we are rarely taught to do that, and our physiology doesn't help us. Our brain's physical inner core evolved early in human development, and it served to keep us physically safe. Our prefrontal cortex developed later as we adapted to a changing world and needed more complex judgment capacity. We end up with fight, flight, or freeze patterns meant for life-threatening encounters like those with saber-toothed tigers and other predators—only today the threats are happening in our workplace. Our brain's physical evolution has not kept up with our modern world. So, these mechanisms in specific contexts are no longer our best friend, keeping us safe, but are often the source of limiting beliefs, unexamined thinking habits, and the creator of blind spots. Our attention focuses on specific ways without our even noticing.

Let's walk through career planning using the modified CBT model.

1. Remember a sabotaging thought that you've had recently about your career, and write it down. Some examples I hear include: "I don't have enough experience for that job." "People don't like me in interviews." "I can't get a job." "I'll never get a better job." "I don't know how to job hunt, so why bother."

2. Write down all the evidence supporting this thought distortion. In what ways is this sabotaging thought true? Keep digging even if you don't believe there's anything genuine about it. There's undoubtedly some grain of truth—it just might take a moment of brainstorming to get there.

3. Write down all the evidence against this thought. In what ways is this sabotaging thought false? Even if you feel this is entirely true, try looking at the idea from a few more angles. Maybe you think your friends are judging you—but do you judge those you care about based on their career histories? (I'm guessing the answer is no.)

4. Review your list. Notice all those false statements? That's why we call these thoughts distortions. We think they're true, but

when it comes down to it, they're mostly false. And now you know how to pick them apart.

For example, last week, Alejandro procrastinated and missed a deadline to submit his résumé.

1. Sabotaging thought: "I'm a failure."
2. Thought distortions:
    a. Labeling—he labeled "failure" on something (himself).
    b. All-or-nothing thinking: he missed a deadline for one submission and decided he was a total failure at everything.
3. Evidence supporting his thought:
    a. This is not the first time he has missed a deadline in his life.
4. Evidence against his thought:
    a. He's already submitted other material in a timely way for different positions.
    b. He has several interviews lined up.
    c. He has a career strategy plan that he has been implementing with updated paperwork and an excellent social media strategy.
    d. This is the first time he has taken a wrong moment and examined it face-to-face without letting it get him offtrack, resorting to unhealthy habits, or giving up.

It turns out we don't only have sabotaging thoughts when we make one mistake; we also have them when we are doing well. Thought distortions pop up for all sorts of reasons:

- Experience. Maybe you've been burned before and are just trying to protect yourself from feeling like a failure again. With a thoughtful career strategy and new mental habits, you can avoid the thought distortions that get us offtrack.
- Fear of failure. Perhaps the thought of failure has always scared you. Use the model to learn how to overcome a mistake or an obstacle.

- Lack of confidence. You may underestimate your abilities and have always felt unsure you could take on a real-life challenge. Now, you are building self-efficacy.
- Low self-esteem. Maybe you don't think much of yourself right now for various reasons. Now, you can work toward goals that will make you proud, or you can review your "happy file" (more on this in chap. 8).
- Fear of success. You may fear what it would feel like to reach your career goals. While living in Japan, I learned the saying, "the nail that sticks out gets hammered down." If success feels both attractive and dangerous, the conflict can keep you frozen. When you are afraid, create, choose, and say statements that describe another reality—your being fully equipped to do your job, and the next one—successfully.

Imposter's syndrome is such a common issue that it deserves special consideration. Imposter syndrome is a psychological phenomenon where people doubt their accomplishments and fear being exposed as a fraud despite evidence of their competence and success. In chapter 1, I described a former client whose imposter thinking caused great suffering. It is a common experience for many people, particularly high-achieving individuals. It is the result of distorted thinking and can lead to feelings of anxiety, self-doubt, and a lack of confidence.

Using the cognitive behavioral techniques regularly can help you bring to awareness the automatic thinking that we all do and give you a choice to think other thoughts that are much more supportive. Take a situation and analyze it by writing down its five key aspects. Your responses will differ for each situation, but the keywords—circumstances, thoughts, feelings, actions, and results—are always the same. This covers the critical aspects of the model:

1. The Circumstance. The circumstance includes the facts of any situation, typically things we could not control. In this model, the circumstances are one sentence that could be factually

confirmed or verified by others. Often, this is the "problem" that you want to address. Write this down as a statement.

2. The Thought. This is the sentence, the words that occur in your mind. The thought is what your brain has told you about the circumstance. It is your brain's interpretation of the facts. It is the meaning that you have attached to the neutral, observable circumstance. Sometimes, it is the mantra that has been repeating in your brain, but sometimes, it is a nugget you must unearth by being quiet and listening carefully as you read the circumstance. After you read the circumstance, what thought shows up? There are often multiple thoughts, but typically, there is a dominant one. It's the one about which you have the most feelings, the most significant reaction. You can separate other thoughts and address them later. Don't try to do too much at one time because it will limit your ability to be surprised.

3. The Feelings. We often have many feelings and emotions that the circumstance is seemingly generating. So, this category is a one-word description of the vibrations in your body caused by the thought. Do a quick body scan, and you should be able to notice at least one feeling that is associated with your thinking. "No feeling" or "numbness" is also an emotional reaction. You may feel nothing, but that is valid and valuable to note. Notice that you are not addressing or focusing on the circumstance; you're looking at what feeling state in your body has been generated by the sentence in your brain that you have told yourself.

4. Actions. Our behavior, actions, and what we do or don't do because of our thoughts and feelings about the circumstance. Write keywords down.

5. Results. These are the consequences that occur because of the actions we did or did not take. They are what happened when

we did or did not choose to do something. Our results are the effect or evidence of the initial thought. Write keywords down.

Tables 6.1 and 6.2 are examples from my clients who have experimented with this tool to work on their thought distortions. One of my clients started with the problem statement, "I hate my job" (table 6.1). Because this is a feeling statement, it goes into the feeling category. From that designation you can build up or down. Identify what you think is a problem related to your career. Then, place the statement in one of the categories.

I recommend choosing the dominant, most critical, most important thought (T), feeling (F), action (A), and result (R). Still, it is helpful to download everything the first time you start exploring the circumstance. Then, you will want to circle the T, F, A, and R that has the most juice or seems the most important. Table 6.2 is an example of an unintentional model created by a client, this time starting with the problem statement, "I'm nervous about an upcoming interview."

I call the above models "unintentional" because it is our thoughts that have been driving our feelings, actions, and results without being conscious of that dynamic. Now that you know this dynamic, you can decide that a particular thought no longer serves you. Whatever past context in which that thought was created, such as a parent's voice or your inner child's interpretation, you can decide to think something else. Sounds easy, but turning unintentional thoughts into intentional

Table 6.1. The Five Key Aspects of a Sample Problem: "I Hate My Job"

Circumstance	I have had this job for over six years.
Thought	I am stuck, with no way to dig myself out of this hole.
Feelings	I feel depression, anger, sadness, and lack of energy, but the dominant feeling is hopelessness.
Actions	Complaining, drinking too much alcohol, sleeping, and eating too much.
Results	No energy for job hunting.

Table 6.2. The Unintentional Model: "I'm Nervous about an Upcoming Interview"

Circumstance	I have a job interview scheduled for next Monday.
Thought	There is no way I can sufficiently prepare for their aggressive questioning.
Feeling	Anxiety
Actions	Cancel the interview
Results	Still job hunting
Circumstance	My to-do list includes doing two informational interviews with senior staff in my preferred organization.
Thought	I'm uninteresting, introverted, and too junior to take their time. I don't deserve any attention.
Feeling	Intimidated, anxious
Actions	Never make the calls
Results	Professional network not expanded

ones or reframing the thought requires practice and more healing. I've included in Appendix A some space to practice your own models. I suggest making copies as this is a tool you can use many times over.

When creating an intentional model, keep the same circumstance and insert a new thought. Using these three examples, intentional thoughts might be:

"I can learn to create an action plan that will move me, step by step, to a new job."
"I can prepare for an interview and I trust that all the answers are already within me."
"I am a respectful, intelligent person genuinely curious and grateful for some time with these professionals."
"I am confident that I bring value to this organization."

In the beginning, the thought you choose, with intention, may feel foreign and fake, but take some time to say it to yourself and let it settle in. Keep repeating and practicing the new thought. When the intentional thought takes hold, use the model to see if new actions and results begin to emerge. Everything shifts inside as you allow a great sense of hope, empowerment, confidence, and relaxation to settle in. You deserve it.

Another critical aspect of this model is that it teaches us that we can live through uncomfortable feelings, rather than beating ourselves up about them. We do a lot to avoid those feelings we identify as uncomfortable, but the fact is that even failure itself is just a mental construct.

I often list the five items and write something down for each item as a five-minute morning activity; part of my mindful practice includes meditation and gratitude journaling. It is easier for me to complete the "feeling" statement and then work up and down the model. It is beneficial to use this model especially upon waking up with heavy feelings left over from dreaming, turning to the model immediately. It's a great way to clear the air so that those heavy feelings don't dominate the day. Spend five minutes every morning doing a "thought download" and a meditation practice. I write down all the random thoughts going on in my brain. Putting things on paper helps me get them out of my head, slow them down, bring them up to an awareness, and look at the process from my awake, inner observer perspective. I still write the model down, although I've been known to think something through using the model while in the grocery checkout line. You can enter the model from any category.

Analyzing your situation via this model will strengthen your inner observer because what you are doing as you write down your response is noticing how your thinking affects not only your feelings but also your behavior and the results you get in life. This simple tool can work on every aspect of your life—your habits, relationships, and career. You can use the content in Appendix A to develop your own model.

Look at the model you've developed and reflect on these questions:

- How do I feel when I think this thought?
- How do I act when I think this thought?

- What is the result of my actions when I think this thought?
- What if I learned how to experience that uncomfortable feeling while making different choices in my thinking about it?

It's a beautiful moment when you decide that a particular thought no longer serves you. You wish it well for what your brain tried to do to protect you, but make a conscious decision to think of something more supportive and empowering that does not generate the negative emotions that you may have become accustomed to. Yes, we can choose our thoughts, but they require continued, mindful practice as the neural pathways reroute in new ways. Once they take hold, you'll be surprised by how your feelings change, and all possible actions come to mind.

By acknowledging negative self-talk, individuals can learn to identify and challenge those thoughts and beliefs contributing to living lesser lives. Strategies that have proven helpful in addressing thought distortion include:

1. Reframing negative self-talk. Replacing self-critical thoughts with more positive and realistic ones can involve challenging negative thoughts and beliefs with evidence and logic.

2. Developing a more realistic view of success. Recognizing that setbacks and failures are a normal part of the learning process, and that success is not always perfect, can help us better understand the true nature of reaching our goals.

3. Seeking support from others. Sharing experiences with trusted friends, family, or a mental health professional in a safe space allows us to talk about the persistent thoughts. It is an effective way of receiving validation and support. Also, seeking feedback from trusted sources can help us gain a more accurate understanding of our strengths.

4. Focusing on strengths. Making the choice to focus on our personal strengths and accomplishments, rather than on areas

that need improvement, can help us build confidence and reduce feelings of self-doubt.

5. Developing self-compassion. Practicing compassion and kindness toward ourselves can help us recognize our worth and value, and learn to accept and celebrate our successes.

6. Practicing self-care. Engaging in activities that promote physical and mental well-being—such as exercise, meditation, or spending time in nature—help set the context in our lives for success.

7. Setting realistic goals. Setting achievable goals and celebrating small successes can help us build confidence and reduce feelings of inadequacy.

CHAPTER 7

Goal Setting

- What stepwise process can I use to create goals that plug the gaps I've identified while working toward my vision?

You did intense work in chapter 6, working through Steps 1 through 5, and now you will use all that insight to turn the identified gaps into a set of goals. Goals matter because they empower performance. Now that you have goals that build the bridge to your vision, it's time to implement the game plan, the mechanics of seeking and finding your next professional position. The rest of this book will guide you in the critical best practices of job hunting: burnishing your paper story, curating your online presence, strengthening your professional network, and improving your interpersonal interactions with potential employers (interviewing, callbacks, check-ins). Most people think this is the core of job hunting, but you've already done the foundational work upon which all else rests.

Step 6 is to turn that list of gaps into a plan—a series of goals, the why of each goal, and the implementation plan. You create goals to close the difference between where you are now and your vision. A big vision can usually be divided into a series of goals. Develop a list of goals for the next twelve months (this exercise comes from Lindsay Satterfield, my productivity coach). Writing down goals to increase the likelihood of accomplishing them is essential. Now, revisit each goal and develop a list of why that goal is meaningful to you. Writing down the "why" of each goal will help strengthen your focus. When the inevitable obstacles occur, including the waning of energy for your plan, you have a written document you can revisit to remind you why these goals mattered in the first place.

So far, you have analyzed global health trends and key competency clusters, reviewed the descriptions of the jobs you find desirable, and identified vital knowledge, attitudes, experience, and skill gaps as well as thought distortions that you would like to address. You know that addressing these things will contribute to your future self—your vision. Now that you have a clearer sense of that vision, it is time to develop the goals that are your specific pathway to that vision. You create the goals that will help you reach the picture you created of your future self as it relates to your professional life. Although this process would work for all the aspects of your vision, my examples will focus on your professional life.

If your vision is a picture of your future self, your goals are the pathway. Edwin Locke and Gary Lathram, known for their goal-setting theory, studied high performers to decode their secrets. It's not just a genetic predisposition. High performers' secrets are transferable to others. The secrets can be learned, and that's good news for the rest of us.

Consider establishing a date—perhaps one year from now—and develop the professional goals that will move the needle toward your vision along that timeline. Latham and Locke's goal-setting theory proposes that setting specific and challenging goals can enhance motivation, performance, and productivity. Like visioning, the theory suggests that various factors influence goal setting and effectiveness. The following factors will increase the chances that your goals support the vision and are more likely to succeed. Create goals that are:

1. Clear and specific. It's essential to be as detailed as possible because the more precise your goals are, the more likely you are to keep them in mind. Clear and specific goals are more effective

than vague or general ones. Setting objectives provides a clear direction and enhances motivation.

2. Important to you. The perceived importance or relevance of your goals to your individual values and aspirations will help provide motivation and effort in pursuing your goals. Using your vision as the guiding light will align your goals with your values.

3. Owned and committed to. Goals are more likely to be achieved when you oversee the goal-setting process and have a sense of ownership and commitment to the goals. Don't let someone else do this work for you, not even a coach or family member.

4. Achievable. Believing in your capabilities (self-efficacy) and working to develop necessary skills and resources play a significant role in goal achievement. Individuals with higher self-efficacy tend to set more challenging goals and persist in facing obstacles.

5. Challenging. There is nothing wrong with "stretch" goals, which can lead to higher effort and performance than easily attainable goals. But goals should still be achievable, helping you maintain motivation and commitment. The best goals are both feasible and challenging. You are more likely to accomplish a difficult goal than an easy one (what is referred to as a "low goal"). A sense of risk heightens focused efforts and engagement. In addition, as you progress on challenging goals, you gain confidence and a sense of efficacy, setting in motion a reinforcing loop of accomplishment. Going for only the easy goals can ensnare you in the trap of complacency. That said, you also want to avoid goals that look impossible.

6. Tracked. Getting regular feedback on your progress toward goals is crucial for motivation and performance. Set up a tracking system, including reminders in critical places.

7. Magnetic. Consider at least one goal that inspires and is exciting to you. It draws you in and captures your imagination. "Approach" goals take you positively toward something. "Avoidance" goals act like repellent, taking you away from an outcome. Approach goals tap into positive emotions, stimulating the brain's learning centers, while avoidance goals stir negative emotions, which can stifle or paralyze action. In goal setting, we sometimes end up with the result we try to avoid because we are focused on what we don't want. Also, if you need to accomplish a professional goal that does not inspire you, is there a way to revise it to make it more magnetic or meaningful? Emotional engagement with a goal aids with its accomplishment.

8. Known to others. Imagine sharing your vision with people you know and trust. Saying it out loud is a way of inviting people to support the way the process will unfold, often a challenging line. Sharing your vision and the current goal supports your commitment. Accountability is a powerful driver of behavior change. While committing yourself through writing them down is effective and helps amplify accountability, making your goals visible to others packs an even greater punch.

Consider developing a goal for each of the significant KASE gaps you identified. Address the best practices of goal setting, such as your goals being clear, specific, and doable. Consider three to five goals at a particular time. Keep your vision in mind and follow this process for each goal:

1. Define your objective. State your goal in a way that will be clear when you have achieved it. What will be accurate? How will it be observable or verifiable? Identify what you want to accomplish. Make it specific, measurable, achievable, relevant, and time-bound (SMART). Write it as if it has already happened. Instead of "I want to get a job," a SMART goal would be, "In December, I am employed by an organization that meets my three criteria:

making X salary, in X country, and focusing on X activities." Adjust this exercise to address whatever your professional priorities are.

2. Break it down. Divide your main goal into smaller, manageable steps or milestones. James Clear, author of *Atomic Habits,* is not a fan of goals but does emphasize attention to the small, most-likely-to-be-successful habits that support incremental change over time. This makes it easier to track progress and stay motivated. Each milestone should be specific and have a deadline. For instance, if your main goal is to address a competency gap in technology, your milestones could include identifying the most sought-after technologies, finding the best courses or certifications programs, signing up for the course/program, completing it, graduating, sharing your achievement with your professional network and on social media, and adding it to your résumé.

3. Set a timeline. Determine the time frame in which you want to achieve your goal. Setting a deadline creates a sense of urgency and helps you stay focused. Consider the complexity of your goal and the time you can realistically commit. Break down your milestones into smaller deadlines, ensuring they align with your primary goal's timeline.

4. Identify obstacles. Anticipate potential challenges or obstacles that may hinder your progress. It could be a lack of time, resources, or external factors. Identify these barriers in advance so you can develop strategies to overcome them. This could involve seeking support from others, acquiring additional skills, or adjusting your plan.

5. Write and post. Writing down goals is positively correlated with attaining them. According to research by Gail Matthews, there is a 42 percent advantage because writing creates and fortifies a new mental circuit. In her study, 149 participants were randomly

sorted into various groups with different instructions regarding their goal planning. Besides the positive effects of accountability and public commitment, participants who wrote their goals accomplished significantly more than those who did not write down their goals. The act of writing by hand provides extra cognitive reinforcement. Keep your goals visible and reference them regularly. Writing your goals supports something known as "precommitment." You are putting a stake in the ground, and the visual cue keeps the goals on your mind, strengthening these mental circuits.

6. Create an action plan. For each goal, outline the specific actions you need to take to achieve each milestone. Be detailed and include the necessary resources, skills, and tasks. Prioritize these actions based on their importance and sequence. A well-defined action plan makes your goal more manageable and provides a road map for progress.

7. Track your progress. Regularly monitor and evaluate your progress. Set up checkpoints to review your milestones and adjust your approach if necessary. Track measurable metrics related to your goals, such as Tableau software certification, identifying three preferred organizations, implementing at least six networking activities. Celebrate small victories along the way to maintain motivation.

8. Stay motivated. Maintain your enthusiasm and motivation throughout the goal-setting process. Find ways to stay inspired, such as visualizing success, seeking support from friends or mentors, or rewarding yourself for reaching milestones. Stay committed and focused on why you set the goal in the first place.

Setting a goal is an essential next step. Taking consistent action, adapting to challenges, and staying motivated are vital to achieving your professional goals. Below are some examples of how the steps outlined above may apply to goal setting for professional advancement.

Vision: In 2030, I am a published senior technical expert in maternal health, managing a five-year funded project focusing on young mothers and infants.

By month 20XX, I will have earned an advanced degree.

By month 20XX, I will live in my desired country/continent and work in a health-related position.

By month 20XX, I will have published at least one research study.

By month 20XX, I will be presenting my results at a professional conference.

By month XXXX, I will become certified in Tableau.

In chapter 4, you did a deep dive, exploring your current situation through various perspectives. That analysis forms the baseline of your personal and professional status in ways that influence your everyday professional life. In chapter 5, you fleshed out a vision for your future. You developed this vision by analyzing what is in your best interest, alone or considering significant others. In chapter 6, you did a gap analysis, influencing the next step in the process: goal setting. I advise that you develop annual goals, with each goal broken down into two sets of six-month goals. Then, use each six-month goal to generate a realistic set of calendared actions and milestones. Developing a three-month timeline creates an easier, more realistic path, and you can embed victory moments that help you keep the momentum going.

Remember, you are now a strategic thinker managing a lifelong career strategy with a large vision, so you may not be building a profile for the next job but for the job after that or after that. Frank, one of my former clients, told me early on that his goal was to be the director of the Peace Corps. For now, that is his big vision. He was using his Harvard PhD in public health to go deeply into infectious disease research, where he was consistently a valued, popular team member. Although he was searching for a subsequent position in global health, I connected him with a former Peace Corps director friend for an informational interview. I asked him to review some of the histories that had been written about former Peace Corps directors. He realized that he would need to pay much more attention to creating political connections over time, but in the immediate future, he needed additional management and senior leadership experience. So, Frank has a dual focus—his immediate next job and how that job contributes to a pathway toward a significant leadership role. Fate may keep him from a political appointment, but it won't be because he didn't follow a vision or gather skills and experience toward that vision. For the next job, it became clear that he would prioritize management roles in a way he had not previously.

It's also helpful to foster a relationship with an accountability partner, someone you know, trust, and can check in with. An accountability partner can help keep you on track without shaming or judgment. An excellent professional friend can serve that role. I serve this role with clients who now see me as a trusted lifetime advisor and contact me when they feel stuck or want a higher-level review.

As a savvy career strategist, you will check in on and fine-tune your planning for the rest of your professional life, repeating this process occasionally. Sometimes, the dream job is different from what you envision, but the next role you can set yourself up to reach your goal. That is why strategic career planning is so critical to success. I recommend an annual checkup on your career strategy, using the tools in this book to do that work.

- **PART III**

GOAL GETTING

Implementing the Plan

CHAPTER 8

Creating Your Professional Records System

- What paperwork filing system can I create to make life easier as my career progresses?
- What's the latest in what works in résumés and cover letters?

Calling all packrats and hoarders! Here is one topic that may warm your hearts because it is often the top-of-mind concern of the job hunter. This chapter is about organizing paperwork to help you manage your career over your entire professional life. The first big idea to get your head around is a resource system that you will use consistently rather than dusting off the old résumé only when job hunting.

Remember the mindset of running a business of one? Even if you are happy in your current work, you don't want to ignore or, even worse, not know about opportunities to meet your evolving needs. It is not disloyal to keep abreast of other opportunities. Knowing what's out there and deciding to stay is one of the most empowering spaces for anyone. Don't wait to hate your job before you start looking. Sometimes, a good job is the enemy of the best job.

You think you'll never forget the work you did or the successes you had, but you will. When you need to document something for future employment, you cannot remember the details of your work, the effort you made, and the results you achieved. But after you use this system, you'll find it easy to access your work history. A system like this puts all the information you need at your fingertips, retrievable whenever you need it. In a rare situation where something becomes a legal matter, this information will be easy to locate. Finally, it's excellent material for your memoirs and your biographer. (Hey, you never know!) I didn't start this system until midcareer and wish I was able to recall a particular story or the year it happened.

The documents we are talking about are:

- The happy file
- Professional paperwork
- Curriculum Vitae
- Résumés
- Cover letters

The sooner you create this system in your career, the more valuable it will be to you over time. It will save you time and lost opportunity and provide access to your complete, organized, professional story. But even if you're getting a late start, it's not too late to retrieve and organize these precious documents. I confess that I am somewhat "old school." I like the physical files, but creating an electronic version is a good idea, as it can become extensive. An electronic filing system is easier to search, too. Keep the documents virtually on your computer, scanning them as they come in—or simply store them in your preferred manner. We will explore additional communications in chapter 11 (interviewing, callbacks, and check-ins).

Item 1: The Happy File

The happy file (or whatever you want to call it) includes every positive thing you have heard or received regarding yourself as a professional. Every complimentary email or letter goes into that file, ensuring any numerical data are apparent. If you receive copies of recommendations, they also go into this file. Start doing this now, and if the file becomes significant, you can organize the contents by date or by job. I started my file in counseling graduate school, where we were learning how to facilitate small groups. One of the joint exercises at the end of retreats was called "strength bombardment." Each had paper taped to their back. The instructions were to write something positive about each person on their paper. Everyone was included, ending the exercise with a page full of personal, positive comments. That piece of paper was one of the first things I put in my happy file. You should also include congratulatory comments that describe something specifically appreciative or complimentary about your professional life. Anything positive that comes to you about you in letters, emails, or performance evaluations should go into your happy file. Keep in mind that it should not include nice comments from family members about your character and good work. Your happy file documents your professional self and provides concrete examples of how others experience you.

The usefulness of the happy file becomes apparent when you feel down on yourself, your inner critic has kicked in, or you're having a challenging experience of failure. The happy file is great for those moments when your brain tells you that you are an impostor, unworthy, or not good at your job. Open the file and be reminded of your strengths. Some of the most talented people I know have these dark moments, and in my coaching, I'm amazed by how familiar this aspect of humanity is—the self-doubt, the dark moments of just being human. The quiet drumbeat of "not good enough, not good enough."

According to Dan Siegel and Ann Betz, plenty of neuropsychological research tells us about the brain's negative bias. Negative bias refers to the tendency to pay more attention to and give more weight to negative information than positive information. It can be attributed to a combination of evolutionary and psychological factors, with the brain's neuroplasticity reinforcing thought patterns. This bias can be observed in various aspects of our cognition, such as memory, attention, and decision making. Adverse events and emotions affect us more substantially and are more likely to be remembered and recalled in greater detail. A few reasons for this tendency toward negativity are:

1. Survival instincts. From an evolutionary standpoint, our brains have evolved to prioritize negative information and experiences

as a means of survival. In ancestral times, being attuned to potential threats and dangers was crucial for our ancestors' survival. Negative experiences often carry more immediate and significant consequences for our well-being, so our brains have developed a heightened sensitivity to negative stimuli.

2. Threat assessment. Our brain is wired to constantly scan the environment for potential threats and can't differentiate between a saber-toothed tiger and a toxic work environment. This vigilance toward negative stimuli is known as the "threat assessment" mechanism. It allows us to be more cautious and prepared in potentially dangerous situations. The brain's heightened sensitivity to negative information helps us evaluate risks and take appropriate actions to ensure our safety.

3. Learned experiences. Negative experiences often leave a stronger impression than positive ones. Our brains more easily learn from adverse events to avoid similar situations in the future. This learning process helps us adapt and make better choices to minimize harm or maximize rewards.

While the negative bias served an essential purpose in our evolutionary past, it can sometimes lead to cognitive distortions and emotional imbalances in modern-day life. By understanding this bias, however, we can consciously work toward balancing our perceptions and focusing on positive aspects, fostering a healthier and more balanced mindset. The happy file is a tool you create to address the inevitable moments of self-doubt.

There is that moment when we feel we have failed, but we haven't started to work through it yet to get to the other side. Taking out the happy file and just looking through the pages of positive comments can feed your spirit and remind you that you are not who your brain is telling you that you are now. While writing this chapter, I reviewed my happy file, and it's incredible how this exercise still works, especially when I notice self-doubt creeping in. Over the years, I have improved my ability to identify dysfunctional thinking, but I still need to practice awareness, which is not a one-time choice but a process. See chapter 6 for more information on how our brains are not our best friends and what you can do about it.

Another important reason for a happy file is that you may want to remember who could serve as a suitable reference, and their positive comments fed back to them are the reminder they need to agree to your request. Finally, you may want to use testimonials in your happy file as part of your social media presence in the future.

As an example, the program manager of the Family Planning Association of Kenya (FPAK) wrote the following after I was hired by Johns Hopkins University as a consultant to work in Kenya: "I wish to take this opportunity to thank you sincerely for your effective supervision of the three TOTs [training of trainers] . . . In a nutshell, I would say that your hard work, clear thinking, organization, and counsel are something great to emulate."

JHU's Center for Communication Programs almost immediately hired me as a senior program officer in the Africa Division mainly because of that positive confirmation of my performance in the field from a critical, credible LMIC leader. Thank you, Margaret Thuo, wherever you are. This 1990 document is still in my happy file, and reading it can flip my negative self-talk.

Item 2: Professional Paperwork

Files such as position descriptions, work products, program reports, publications performance evaluations, and company reports support your résumé, which is the synthesized, focused story of your professional successes and experience. By midcareer, your professional story becomes too detailed and complex to be called up quickly. The paperwork in your professional paperwork file should include the following.

1. Job descriptions and scopes of work, from the one used to hire you to the ones that inevitably evolve. Organizations and

managers who ignore job descriptions don't understand their importance in setting agreed-upon expectations that are critical in measuring performance. Even if you are working in an organization that doesn't use job descriptions, keep the advertisement for the position in your file, and before your first evaluation, develop a one-page job description with simple bullets that enumerate what you do and any relevant metrics that might be used to measure your success objectively. Job descriptions are good historical documents but can be utilized to negotiate clarity with employers.

2. Work contracts. Not every job requires a contract, but if yours does, these documents often include scopes of work or the highest-level legal expectations of your activities.

3. Work reports. Examples of work reports are publications describing the company you work for or the program you work in. Often, these reports include the metrics vital to your résumé.

4. Written work products. These are copies of any substantial writing you have done or other content you created. It is important to start documenting your writing or creative abilities early in your career. Any peer-reviewed or other research and program publications with your name listed should be included.

5. Other work products. Additional documentation includes the agenda of events you are listed in, the presentations that involved you, infographics, and any handouts related to your work.

Keeping these items organized will save you time and lost opportunity when highlighting a past activity that reflects your skill and experience and might relate to the position you are applying to.

Item 3: Curriculum Vitae

Even if your jobs thus far have called for résumés only, creating a curriculum vitae (CV) document as your key "cheat sheet" record of your professional life is a good idea. My CV is now my source document. Keeping it updated has been invaluable in helping me track activities and results, dates, and locations.

Curriculum vitae is Latin for "course of life." In contrast, *résumé* is French for "summary." These two documents tell the story of your professional life. The CV is typically a multipage listing of everything you have done. You can create one large CV document that includes work experience like the résumé and academic degrees, teaching experience, research, awards, publications, presentations, and other achievements, skills, and credentials. CVs are typically used for educational, medical, research, and scientific applications in the United States and abroad. The United Nations system and international NGOs will often request them. When I did some work for WHO, they wanted that document. I had already been working professionally for fourteen years before I was required to provide a CV, so I know it is missing some of my early presentations and writings. I regret that because years later, my earlier research experiences in cross-cultural communication became relevant again.

You may be instructed by your potential employer on a specific format they require. Several reliable Internet and AI resources can help you create a CV. Here are a few popular ones:

1. Canva (www.canva.com). Canva is a versatile online design tool offering various templates specifically designed for CVs. It provides a user-friendly interface and allows you to customize your CV with different layouts, fonts, colors, and graphics.

2. Novoresume (www.novoresume.com). Novoresume offers a simple and intuitive CV builder with a wide selection of professionally designed templates. It provides step-by-step guidance and suggestions to help you create a well-structured CV. Some features are available for free, while others require a subscription.

3. Zety (www.zety.com). Zety offers an easy-to-use CV builder that lets you quickly create a professional-looking CV. It delivers a

variety of templates and provides helpful tips and examples for each section of the CV. Zety offers both free and premium options.

4. LinkedIn (www.linkedin.com). LinkedIn is a professional networking platform that allows you to create an online CV. You can input your information directly into your LinkedIn profile and format it accordingly. LinkedIn profiles can serve as an online CV that allows potential employers to find and learn more about you.

5. Microsoft Word and Google Docs. These popular word-processing tools provide numerous CV templates you can customize according to your needs. Both platforms offer a variety of professional-looking templates, making it easy to create and edit your CV.

Item 4: A Résumé Tailored for Each Position

Commonly you will receive requests to provide a résumé, which is a much shorter, more focused document. Your résumé won't get you hired—job interviews do that—but it will screen you out. Respecting the idea that recruiter preferences evolve, I've attached a model many have used successfully in Appendix C.

Step 1. You want to make it easy for recruiters to access essential information. Human resource research indicates that recruiters generally scan a résumé for a few seconds and will look mainly for keywords or criteria that match the job description's keywords. Those are the items you want to stand out in your résumé, which should be basic, easy to read, straightforward, and clean. Just the facts. Do not include any soft skills or subjective adjectives. Focus on your complex, quantifiable skills. This typically means you must compose your résumé with an HIC organization in mind. It no longer works to tout your soft skills or use a lot of adjectives. Social desirability bias research indicates that lengthy or overly detailed résumés are beginning to annoy hiring managers. Your résumé should only communicate your hard skills and experience. Remember to cut all the soft skills unless you can quantify them. Using data and numbers will set you apart from the other résumés. This is not your time to be narcissistic or braggy. Recruiters don't ever really believe all that malarky anyway. They will decide on your interpersonal skills and fit with the organization or team based on the interview, not the résumé. The résumé's only purpose is to get you a call from the recruiter. It is what gets you in the door. The interview is where hiring managers assess your interpersonal skills and determine whether your personality is the right fit for the team and organization. The résumé template in Appendix C meets these criteria.

Recruiters typically have more résumés than they need to get to the next step in the hiring process, so they are reviewing them to put as many in the "no" pile as possible. In its 2018 Eye-Tracking Study, Ladders Inc. revealed that the time recruiters spend on the initial screen of a résumé is up from an average of only 6 seconds in 2012, but only by about a second. Today's recruiters skim résumés for an average of 7.4 seconds. Recruiters preferred résumés that featured simple layouts with clear sections and heading titles.

Studies have shown that people follow specific patterns when reading text on a page. The E-pattern and F-pattern are two common reading patterns. In the E-pattern, the reader scans the page as an "E," focusing on the sides of the top, left, and right. In the F-pattern, the reader scans horizontally across the top and vertically down the page. Résumés organized by either of these patterns did well, especially when they used bold titles and bulleted accomplishments. By organizing your résumé content to align with these patterns, you can ensure that critical information catches the reader's attention.

Getting your résumé in the "yes" pile requires the information to be provided in a certain way or within their computerized format. Follow the stated expectations of each employer, especially government employers who may use one of the hundred-plus applicant tracking systems (ATSs) or automated recruitment systems (ARSs) to scan and remove your résumé if it doesn't meet their required format. You may receive a complex online or paper document to complete. You might also be expected to insert your résumé information into an online document. If you are required to complete an online questionnaire, use your résumé as your guide, provide exactly what they ask for, and do not leave any space blank. This is where your professional paperwork system can be handy, as specific work examples, dates, and countries will be retrievable and make your story more powerful. Sometimes, hiring managers will want you to attach your résumé, and all the rest of this advice relates to that document.

The most often suggested résumé format is as follows (see Appendix C for a sample résumé template).

- Contact information. Name, phone number, LinkedIn profile information, personal website, and any other ways to reach or learn about you. (Be sure not to include any address details.)
- Expertise. List any and all keywords that precisely reflect the job description (think "skills").
- Career highlights. Select a few quantifiable successes that fit the position you are seeking.
- Work history. This is your employment story. Remember to tailor your headline to the specific job you're applying for, and highlight your relevant skills and experiences. Whichever resource you choose, ensure the final résumé is well organized, concise, and visually appealing.
- Degrees. List any degrees earned, disciplines, and schools (do not include grade-point average or years of attendance).
- Other relevant information. If applicable, include languages, technologies, certifications, industries, publications/research, and awards.

The top half of the first page, sometimes called "above the fold," is the prime territory where your most critical, memorable information should go. Professional recruiters such as those in USAID's STAR Program, which recruited global health fellows (the majority were LMIC professionals), have described the importance of this first-impression content. Just be careful not to include so much information that the reviewers skip over it. Unfortunately, many career counselors in academic settings still encourage an extensive list of objectives or over-blown, soft-skill-based, adjective-filled words that recruiters skip. Terms like "dedicated," "highly motivated," "professional," "technical guru," "successful," and the like are all a waste of space. After listing your contact information, you want to create a "headline" section that is tailored to the position for which you are applying.

Regarding the length of a résumé, adhere to whatever the recruiting organization states. If nothing is stated, Jennifer Dogbey, STAR's former director of recruitment and now the deputy of USAID's new program to recruit early career humanitarian relief professionals from minority-serving institutions, suggests one page per ten years of experience, or no more than two pages for each higher degree. But Dogbey also reports that it doesn't matter how long the résumé is if the information is relevant and the document is well written and concise. Don't mention employment gaps older than five years or less than a year. If you do need to mention employment gaps, depending on the actual reason, terms like "personal sabbatical," "family care leave," "travel leave," "relocation leave," "parental leave," or "educational leave" are suitable.

Step 2. After you are satisfied with your résumé and think it meets all the conditions, tailor the keywords to the specific job description at hand. If you are currently not responding to a specific job description, write it for the job that reflects your vision of what you want to do next. Of course, they should be significantly similar, right? Today, most organizations, especially global health organizations, use the Internet to recruit worldwide. The midsized and large organizations use applicant/automated tracking software (ATS) to make collecting and reviewing résumés easier. Someone on the technical recruitment team or in human resources selects five to eight keywords or categories, which go into an algorithm that scans the big job-posting sites such as LinkedIn, Facebook, and Indeed. The recruiters also use these keywords to scan résumés in person. If you don't have those keywords, usually seen in the published job description or scope of work, prominently and clearly in your résumé, it will not be picked up.

After you've done the foundational work in the previous chapters and know what you want, your next job will change how you review job descriptions. Now, you will scan for your crucial knowledge and skill-based words. You need to interpret a secret language in the job description because you will need to use that list of keywords from the job description to create your top-fold "headline."

Scan the job description for skills and keywords, and then circle, categorize, think about, and organize them. They are your critical tool to getting your résumé in the action pile, so they should go at the top. In those headlines, you are incorporating your relevant skills and software. They should contain the bulleted vital words that "speak" to the recruiter and will confirm you are a good fit technically for the job.

Think like a recruiter. Your résumé should be easy to skim and highly readable. The 2018 eye-tracking study found that résumés did not fare well if they had cluttered layouts, a lack of white space on the page, multiple columns, and long sentences. A lack of section or job headers was also a negative, as was a text that didn't flow or draw the eye down the page.

To reiterate, you want to have plenty of white space so the recruiters' eyes can quickly glance through and pick up the key messages. White space helps the recruiter focus their eyes on critical skills. Refrain from expanding the margins to decrease the number of total pages.

Choose fonts that are easy to read and professional. Times New Roman is familiar but has serifs (lines, curls, or tails on the ends of letters), and those slightly complicated symbols are distracting. Instead, use a sans serif font like Arial or Calibri. Use 11- or 12-point type and clean lines with one-inch margins on all sides. Use bolding for your name, key title and headline information, main categories, and, in the work history, your job titles only. Avoid italics and underlining if possible. Too many dots and numbers and font that is too small will make your résumé hard to read. Focus on facts and use one of your most essential tools—white space—rather than the bolding, italics, or underlining. Use numbers, statistics, and data to make your case.

Be brutal about removing unnecessary text. Objectives, professional summaries, and all the hyperbolic text are now content that recruiters will skip over. You will get to share all that information in depth during the interview process.

Recruiters may become defensive when you've overhyped yourself. Any interpersonal, entrepreneurial, or soft-skill areas they say they want are significant, but they like to judge those things for themselves. Since emotional intelligence and attitudinal content are almost impossible to prove in a document, you save precious space when you remove all your soft skills, subjective words, and adjectives from your résumé. Instead, focus on your hard skills, the technical skills that can be quantified. You should use numeric data, which is more accessible for the human eye to read, and carries more weight. In any way that you can, accurately quantify your experience, such as communicating the size and depth of your evaluation. Ratings are more impactful than adjectives like "excellent." You want to communicate results, simplifying and quantifying your experience as much as possible.

Remember that your goal is to get your résumé into the "yes" pile based on a reviewer's quick six- to nine-second scan. Let's talk about formatting because it's so critical. People want to put too much content into their résumé. You want to make it easy for the recruiter to see you have the hard skills and qualifications but also to be intrigued and want to contact you. The recruiter cannot take all these details in, so if your résumé is complicated, hard to read, or dense, they may determine you're either overqualified or, if the keywords are not obvious, underqualified.

Instead of writing long paragraphs, use bullet points to highlight your accomplishments and critical skills, which allows for quick and easy scanning. Bulleted points draw attention and make it easier for hiring managers to grasp your achievements, qualifications, and experiences quickly. They provide a concise and impactful way to showcase your abilities and accomplishments in an easily digestible format. When looking at your source document and your CV, include only those bullet points that support your experience relevant to the position you want. Identifying your accomplishments with metrics is more valuable than talking about your responsibilities.

The work history section of your résumé should include, at most, three to seven bullets for each role, with each bullet being at most two lines, according to research published by the Society for Human Resource Management (SHRM). Having one line per bullet is better. So, you can imagine that having dense text paragraphs could take your résumé out of consideration altogether. Another concept to consider is including problems, solutions, and results (PSRs). Most résumés list what people did, but you can stand out by including a bullet on the problem you solved and some data on the results. This is another way of articulating the value you bring to the new employer and showing the impact of your accomplishments.

Using boldface titles for each section of your résumé helps make the structure clear and allows hiring managers to quickly identify the different sections, such as "Professional Experience," "Education," or "Skills." They create a visual hierarchy, making it easier for the reader to navigate the document and find the relevant information they're looking for.

Timing is also relevant. You want to be one of the first candidates to apply. ATSs vary depending on the algorithms they run, but they are sometimes programmed to stop at a certain number of "qualified" résumés. For this reason, you should apply for a position as soon as it is posted.

Your résumé must prove your value in the desired role. Global health careers almost universally now rely on web-based recruitment processes. But the research tells us that one of the most common ways to win the job is to use your professional network, an essential skill that I discuss in chapter 10. In the distribution of your résumé, be sure to follow all of the employer's procedures and insert the job description's keywords in your skill set just in case they are using any of the ATSs.

But sometimes automated systems make mistakes. So, it's also helpful and not obnoxious to email your résumé to someone senior in the organization or part of the relevant technical team, perhaps the technical leader of that team. It is even better if they are on the hiring team. Doing this will ensure that you're not entirely dependent on the organization's human resources personnel to seriously consider your résumé. This is where you use your professional network to identify someone to whom you could send a cover email and résumé.

If you're interested in an organization but want to learn more about the people who work there, some websites can help you. As I write this chapter, one such website is www.hunter.io, which can assist you in identifying email addresses. Remember that your résumé and cover letter should always be sent as two separate PDF documents so the recruiters don't have to scroll down to read the content therein.

In addition to omitting subjective or overblown descriptions, don't insert photos, multiple colors, icons, emojis, multiple complex formats, dense bullets, or "fill-bars," which are the latest trend and a big waste of space. Fill bars are text boxes that include data or highlighted content. Most recruiters find them frustrating to read. I am sad to report that you must also avoid being overly humorous or clever. Who knows if the recruiter and you share the same sense of humor? You should also refrain from including your home address, an objective, old jobs (if you had responsibilities that are still relevant, limit them to one line), dates beyond the past ten to fifteen years, jargon, acronyms, initials, anything that isn't a fact, fibs, and social media that isn't relevant to your job search.

I've provided much information based on my global health employer experience and the latest research and best practices described in various human resource publications. In truth, however, the many HR recruiters and career advisers out there may have different perspectives and opinions. It's always a good idea to customize your résumé for the position you're applying for. A generic résumé gets filtered out. Combining these strategies allows you to create a visually appealing and well-organized résumé that aligns with how hiring managers typically read and process information. Increase your chances of getting noticed by highlighting the important details, helping the reader quickly identify your essential qualifications and achievements. Taking the steps outlined above will help you make a solid case for your candidacy.

Finally, I will comment on references the potential employer may contact to confirm information and provide opinions regarding your suitability for the position. Although you want to provide anything the potential organization requires in their job announcement, you should generally leave your references off your résumé. It is a waste of space and too early for you to share that information. When the time comes to provide references, you should carefully consider a few different features before sharing their contact information.

1. Be confident that they will say positive things about you.
2. Select a supervisor or someone who has authority over you in doing the type of work you are applying for.
3. Ensure that it has been a short time since they worked with you. It will make the new employer nervous if your references are more than a few years old.

It is vital that your references can confirm what your potential new employer is seeking. At the point they are requesting references, your potential employer is no longer looking for ways to weed you out. You are the choice or one of the best and final, so they have committed. They are now positively biased and looking for ways to confirm the match. The human resources people are seeking confirmation that they made a good choice in bringing you to the attention of the technical hiring team. So, make it easy for them by selecting references who can speak in an informed way about what you did that will resonate with the kind of work the new employer wants you to be able to do.

Again, select references who will say positive things about you, your performance, and working with you. Years ago, I was seeking a senior director for a project I was running. I knew the final candidate professionally and personally and thought she would be great. Using a panel approach, we got to the point of contacting references for the final two candidates. But our first choice's reference said that although she was brilliant with many positive qualities, he also told stories of her out-of-control temper and shared a time when she threw a book at him. This was the death knell of her candidacy because my home office and project culture would never tolerate such behavior. It was a massive lesson in the importance of selecting your references wisely. Only some people are going to have recent supervisors and guaranteed positive comments. Sometimes, we leave a job because we don't like the person we worked for (this is the number one reason for departures in the United States), or we don't want them to know that we are job hunting. It is an appropriate statement to make that you do not wish your current employer to be contacted.

Item 5: Cover Letter

According to Astin Belcak of Cultivatedculture.com, 74 percent of employers say they don't read cover letters, but 53 percent prefer candidates who submit them. The purpose of a résumé is to get the recruiter to contact you. As clear and data driven as the résumé needs to be, the cover letter is another story. The cover letter, sent as a separate PDF, serves a different purpose. Advice about an effective cover letter has shifted dramatically in the past ten years. Today, the cover letter must be personal, compelling, and ignite curiosity, including storytelling components and an "a-ha" moment that shows you deeply understand the potential new employer's work environment.

Remember that recruiters are human beings slogging through many résumés and cover letters, and they are typically looking for a compelling package that they can present to the hiring group or the hiring manager. They may have read hundreds of cover letters. Their eyes go glassy over statements like "I'm interested in the position" or "It's a perfect match for me." They also see many cover letters that say something along the lines of "Here's what you said you wanted, and here's what I've done."

Set aside a rather old-school way of talking about yourself and thinking about who is hiring you. This cover letter is the document where you want to make a personal connection with whomever is reading it. Its purpose is the opposite of the résumé. Effective cover letters often contain three messages, in three paragraphs:

Message 1. A personal connection to the organization. This is where you show that you've researched the company. You can quote its mission and values statements. Give examples of your knowledge and experience with the company you want to work for. Why do you like them? Why would you like to work for them? What do you admire about them? No one is immune to hearing their organization described positively. Make this personal and authentic. If you want to work there, specific reasons should say something about the company and you. Remember your vision? How does this job description and company information fit that?

Message 2. Prove that you can bring value to the organization. You could tell the story of a problem you solved for past employers, how you enjoyed the challenge, how successful you were, and why you're motivated to do this for your following employer/organization. This is where you can strut your stuff as a problem solver. Provide an example of your producing results that would be valuable to the organization.

Message 3. End your cover letter with a statement, a call to action, that you would love to join this organization, their team, or work with this group. Include your email address and phone number in the last paragraph, thank them for their time, and let them know you look forward to hearing from them.

I hope I've made a persuasive case that *now* is the time to create your professional records system of your happy file, your work records, CV, résumé, and cover letter. I also want to stress the importance of these documents being perfect grammatically. I have seen CVs, résumés, and cover letters from LMIC health professionals that were so poorly written it seemed the applicants were not fluent in English when they in fact were. Unfortunately, candidates are often not selected because of simple mistakes that get their documentation tossed into the "no" pile. This is especially true if the position includes writing emails, memos, and reports. At the very least, have your materials reviewed by a native speaker of the language of the organization you want to join. I know it's not fair, but it's the truth. Why let a simple review step keep you from moving forward in your career?

This chapter explored the ecosystem of documents in your career strategy. We investigated the happy file, professional paperwork, CVs, résumés, and cover letters. Consider reviewing and updating these documents once a year, perhaps around the time of your performance evaluation. Making an investment in this system early on and maintaining it will make it easier for you to be one of the first applicants for the job, showing up with the most robust application.

CHAPTER 9

Your Online Presence

- Do I need to use social media in my business-of-one concept, and which platform is most used by recruiters?
- What are the best practices for creating a LinkedIn profile that stands out to recruiters and headhunters?
- Which are the leading Internet sites where employers post positions?

According to Gallup, most professionals, including the American working population, have a close relationship with technology. They grew up with the Internet, and they understand storytelling and communication in unexpected ways. Whether you are a coding master with accounts on X, TikTok, Instagram, YouTube, LinkedIn, and Facebook, or you are a senior professional who has avoided using social media, now is the time to curate an online presence and become adept at using online job posting sites to your benefit. In this chapter, we will discuss both. Your online presence is an essential personal branding tool, giving you either a competitive advantage or betraying your greatest weakness. LinkedIn (www.linkedin.com) is where I suggest you put most of your focus. It is a leading professional networking platform that serves as a job search and recruitment site. It allows job seekers to create profiles, connect with professionals, and search for job opportunities. Employers and recruiters often use LinkedIn to post job listings and find suitable candidates. That said, other websites also have ways to join and create an online presence that increases your opportunity to be seen by global health recruiters. Do not overuse AI, as dependency will keep your unique identity from showing through in all your materials, including your social media.

As the world's largest professional network, LinkedIn has over 930 million members in more than 200 countries and territories. Its stated vision is to "Create economic opportunity for every member of the global workforce." It's also one of the more professional settings; it is the only social media site that I recommend to contain your professional profile.

Go to www.linkedin.com and check out other sites as a comparison. Think about what you like and don't like. Consider reviewing personal sites from a recruiter's perspective. Everyone's site is a virtual résumé, so what is the story or the "brand" that sites communicate? What do you think works or doesn't work?

Your public profile is what people see when they are not connected to you (like most recruiters, headhunters, and future employers). You can control what people see by clicking the pencil icon on the "Public profile & URL" tab on the right side of your profile. In full disclosure, technology is constantly improving, so I'm sharing the approach I'm currently using with my clients. As new websites emerge and LinkedIn develops new features, adjustments must be made. The takeaway message, however, should be to have some social media presence, which recruiters and headhunters use. Right now, the most used site is LinkedIn. Consider it a huge search engine for employers.

If you don't have a profile, follow this chapter's advice and the guidance on the LinkedIn website to create one. Have your résumé on hand; you can transfer most of your content directly to the website. If you've updated your résumé but your Internet profile doesn't match, be sure to update your profile. They must be the same. Some recruiters will double-check as a matter of course. From your LinkedIn profile, you will see a checklist of items on the right side of your screen. If you don't want to show something to people who aren't connected to you yet, "uncheck" that item from the list. I recommend having most if not all of these boxes checked and available for people to see.

Check to see if you've customized your LinkedIn URL to make it easier to remember. For example, just your name and not anything too long will look better on résumés, business cards, emails, and the like. Click the pencil icon on the "Public profile & URL" tab to check your URL link. Too much information may result in it not being read, but if you provide too little, it won't get found.

The "top fold" résumé information, which we discussed in chapter 8, is similar on LinkedIn. Optimizing your profile means addressing the highlights of your profile, your photo, and your keywords headline. Keywords are essential because they make finding you on LinkedIn easier for people (especially recruiters). Remember the applicant/automated tracking systems we explored in chapter 8? They are even more important when it comes to LinkedIn. Recruiters pay the system to pick you out based on a keyword search. If you have the right words, the search will pick you up and bring you to the attention of the recruiter who paid LinkedIn for the service. The keywords often need to be an exact match, however, so pay special attention to the job announcement and ensure those are the words to use. If you showcase the right keywords and use them enough throughout your profile, your profile will appear higher in searches for those keywords. This is how recruiters seek applicants for the jobs they are trying to fill. The more optimized your profile is, the easier it will be for them to find you. This means that your profile is not static; it is best if you interact with and update it regularly. I have found that the best LinkedIn profiles have keywords in the following sections:

- Headline: includes your photo, a background, and the two inches or so of content immediately under your photo
- About
- Activity: if you are engaged on LinkedIn, the algorithm will keep your profile more visible
- Experience
- Education
- Projects: only use this category if you are early career or want to include volunteer work

- Skills
- Publications: if you have them
- Language: if that is part of your story
- Endorsements/Recommendations: nice to include but not necessary; the LinkedIn algorithm does take notice of these
- Interests

In the beginning, you can draw critical words from your professional history. Review your hard and soft skills, technologies you've worked with, and other words that resonate with global health. Think about the skills required for the next job you are targeting (job posts and descriptions). Make the list, and compare it with what your LinkedIn profile currently says. Remember, there are industry-specific hard skills, complex skills that can be applied to various industries, and soft skills (character traits). Don't forget to include technologies, such as the software, tools, and platforms you are proficient in.

Any good LinkedIn profile needs a photo. To edit your profile picture, click on the circular photo. You can also set your visibility settings here, and I recommend you put it to "everyone." The image should be current, well-lit, and facing straight ahead, with no other people/pets in it. Smile and look directly at the camera. The priority for your headshot is that you look approachable and professional. If you are still uncertain, check out www.photofeeler.com, which is a website where you can upload several pictures and others will rate you based on several traits. It is valuable feedback on how you are coming across in your photos. Remember, your image should be well-lit without a lot of distractions in it. It's ok to use your smartphone or to stand against a neutral wall. Just shoot for welcoming, amicable, friendly, and accessible. You know, the kind of person someone wants to work with on their team.

Include the job title that best reflects your professional identity—where you want to go, not your current job title unless that reflects what you want in your next position. Next, list your top skill sets and specific keywords relating to your industry or job. Your current company name can be optional. Consider four to five critical complex skill sets that back up your work experience. It also helps with visual brands—skills you use and want to use in your next opportunity. The text should not be overly distracting—no images and no grandstanding. The same rules for the résumé apply to your LinkedIn profile.

Separate the keywords of your highlight section with hard lines (just hit the shift and dash or underscore keys on your keyboard). Ignore the prompt to select "open to work" or "currently employed." The "headline" is the uppermost section directly under your photo. It includes a title and a small area for text. The headline is your chance to envision and announce your future. One tip is to change the position of the keywords every month or so. LinkedIn's algorithm will take note, and you will move back up the search system. (Or so I have heard from people in the know.)

Although Microsoft owns LinkedIn, Google tells us that the most relevant content is on the first screen. It was created to make it easy for recruiters, which is where LinkedIn makes most of its income. You are choosing relevant keywords—hard skills, transferable skills. You want those keywords on your profile so you get into the top fifty results. Next, check out the templates when selecting your header images and the scene behind your photo. The background image should complement, not compete with, your profile picture. In the background, avoid text, graphics, icons, cutouts of yourself, and political messages. Even if the employer agrees with your sentiments, employees who are politically active on social media tend to make organizations nervous. It is up to you if you decide not work in any organization that doesn't fully support your voice. Otherwise, save posts about your advocacy work for Facebook, X, or TikTok. Your LinkedIn page should be accessible for a potential employer to understand and absorb, but don't assume employers won't look at your social media. Those college party photos are not for the public.

You can also turn your LinkedIn profile into an instant résumé by creating a PDF of the content. It's an on-the-fly solution in case you need to share a résumé while traveling.

In the About section, don't write about yourself in the third person. Long descriptions don't get read, so keep them short and precise. This is also your brand statement; it should tell hiring managers what you do, how you do it, and what you want to do next. You can also say things like, "I love to solve X problems; here's how I do it. And here is what I want to do next." The purpose of the About section is to get them to scroll on. Their click to see more is your goal because it means they are curious.

LinkedIn reorganizes sections every so often, but there has consistently been a section that calls for your résumé content. This can be titled "Experience." Use the "Add to Profile" button to see drop-down menus that allow you to insert your résumé information. LinkedIn currently gives you Core, Recommended, and Additional drop-down menus. Use your résumé as your guide, matching as closely as possible. Definitely don't use the Test Score or Causes options. Organize your résumé, then copy and paste all the great, bulleted, quantifiable metrics that describe your accomplishments. The sections are self-explanatory, so follow LinkedIn's guidance and pull relevant content from your résumé.

LinkedIn's algorithm considers endorsements, so be sure add all the skills you want to use into your profile. Then identify colleagues or coworkers who would endorse you. It often helps to endorse them first, and then ask for the same in return. It is not the most critical section, but consider building it up over time, as it will rank your profile higher in the algorithm recruiters use.

You can do more on LinkedIn with time, energy, and interest. For example, to help boost your profile, you can invite people to connect with you, customizing your LinkedIn invitation so they understand why you want to connect. You can also make posts on your feed. Posting content every week on LinkedIn can have several potential benefits. For example, although LinkedIn's algorithm is not publicly disclosed, it is generally believed that those who actively engage other users will receive more visibility in the platform's feed. LinkedIn may show your content to a broader audience if your posts generate higher engagement (likes, comments, shares), potentially increasing your reach. Although there may not be explicit rewards for posting frequently on their feeds, posting regularly on LinkedIn has several potential benefits:

1. Increased visibility. Posting regularly can help raise your profile on the platform. Your posts reach a larger audience, including your connections and followers, which can lead to more engagement and visibility for your brand as someone who has the right expertise and experience.

2. Thought leadership. Consistently sharing valuable content, insights, and industry-related information can establish you as a thought leader in your field. This can help you build credibility, attract followers, and create networking opportunities.

3. Engagement and networking. Posting frequently allows you to engage with your connections and followers, encouraging conversations and interactions. Engaging with other professionals on the platform can help expand your network and build relationships with individuals who share similar interests or work in related professions.

Besides an optimized LinkedIn profile, the Internet can be an essential tool in your career strategy when actively seeking new employment. Early on, global health organizations used the Internet to help in the recruitment of qualified candidates. For international positions, various job-posting sites cater to the global health sector and offer job opportunities in different regions and organizations worldwide. It is advisable to regularly check these websites and sign up for email alerts, if offered, to stay updated on the latest job openings and opportunities in global health. Professional networks, associations, and academic institutions focused on global health may also provide valuable employment resources. I've included a list in Appendix B of more sites.

- Devex (www.devex.com/jobs/search). Devex is a leading platform for global development professionals, including those in the global health sector. It offers various job listings, news, and resources related to international development and global health.

- Global Health Jobs (www.globalhealthjobs.com). Global Health Jobs is a dedicated job board for professionals seeking positions in global health. It features job listings from international organizations, NGOs, academic institutions, and other entities in the global health sector.
- Global Jobs (www.globaljobs.org). GlobalJobs.org is a popular job board that covers a wide range of fields related to international development, including global health. It aggregates job listings from various sources, including NGOs, government agencies, and international organizations.
- Idealist (www.idealist.org). Idealist is a platform focusing on social impact and nonprofit work. It features job listings, internships, and volunteer opportunities in various sectors, including global and public health.
- ReliefWeb (relief web. int/jobs). ReliefWeb is a specialized platform focusing on humanitarian and development work. It features job listings, internships, and volunteer opportunities in various sectors, including global health.

Other more general but also useful job-hunting websites include:

- CareerBuilder (www.careerbuilder.com). CareerBuilder is another popular job board with a broad range of listings across various industries. It offers search functionality, résumé upload options, and tools for job seekers to connect with employers.
- Glassdoor (www.glassdoor.com). Glassdoor provides job listings, company reviews, and salary information. It allows job seekers to research companies, read employee reviews, and find job openings. Employers can also post job listings and access candidate profiles.
- Indeed (www.indeed.com). Indeed is one of the most significant job search engines globally. It aggregates job listings from various sources, including company websites, job boards, and

recruitment agencies. Job seekers can search for opportunities, upload résumés, and apply directly through the platform.

- Monster (www.monster.com). Monster is a long-established online job board covering various industries and job types. It offers a platform for employers to post job listings and search for candidates, while job seekers can search and apply for positions.

Since many of us began working in global health, the Internet has become integral to one's career development strategy. It can serve you when you use it to become familiar with organizations doing the kind of work you are interested in, to create your profile on LinkedIn and other websites, and to identify current attractive vacancies. This chapter provides key strategies to help you stand out from others doing similar things. Next, we'll look at developing your professional network. The Internet can help you with this task, but you must take the lead.

CHAPTER 10

Creating a Professional Networking System That Keeps on Giving

- Is networking an essential aspect of strategic career planning?
- Is it possible to foster natural networking that doesn't feel manipulative or awkward?
- How do you plan networking opportunities, establish professional relationships, and ensure mutual benefit?

Networking can be awkward, but professional networks are one of the best ways of finding and getting jobs. According to LinkedIn, 80 percent of jobs are gotten via "warm" referral connections, often a friend of a contact. In this chapter, we'll explore networking, how to create and nurture your network (even virtually), and how to make it a natural extension of your connection to others rather than an activity that feels inauthentic and manipulative. Networking is a critical activity for professional life, an essential aspect of strategic career planning, and a source of support and connection with others. Your professional network has a transactional component: You do something for me, and I do something for you. When it comes to networking, however, consider using the model from chapter 6 to create a new thought about the networking activity. Such reframing is extremely helpful, moving it from a phony, opportunistic interaction to leading the interaction with your authentic curiosity and the goal of mutual benefit. Networking can have an element of emotion, especially when you feel supported, understood, and respected and when you are supporting, understanding, and respecting others. It is up to you how large or intimate you want your network to be, because no matter what advice I give you, your comfort level will dictate what happens in this part of your career-planning strategy. This building step is essential because it relates to your brand, mentor relationships, referrals, references, resources, and connections to a community of like-minded professionals. The actions you take to develop, grow, and sustain your professional networking system will be influenced by contributions to your company and extend to professional organizations, events, and external opportunities. The best professional networking strategy involves combining several tactics and approaches.

Start by being mindful and defining your goals. Think about what you want to achieve through networking. Your goals will change depending on where you are in your career. Whether it's finding the next or a new job, expanding your knowledge of organizations doing the work you are interested in, or seeking mentorship, knowing why you want to invest in a professional network will help you focus your efforts and provide motivation to do what is necessary to create and nurture your professional system. If you are early in your career, consider developing the habits outlined in this chapter during your graduate program and any volunteer experience you might have. Your favorite instructors, fellow students, and program participants are an invaluable part of your professional network that could be lost over the years if you neglect to keep in touch. There is something extraordinary about reaching back to colleagues from your "early days," people who shared an essential period with you.

Build genuine relationships by assuming the importance of mutual benefit. Networking is about building authentic connections. Take a genuine interest in others, listen actively, and offer your support and expertise when appropriate. Focus on building mutually beneficial relationships rather than solely seeking personal gain. If your network is entirely one-sided, it won't last long. Networking that is too transactional isn't balanced. Maybe you are shy or introverted, or you go blank. Over the years, I've attended countless events and still provide informational interviews when asked. My heart goes out to the person staring blankly at me, forgetting their "making a good impression" strategy. Or when they try to mask their nervousness with overenthusiasm and bravado. I see them with a drink in their hand, looking wistfully at the exit sign, wondering how long they need to stay. Nowadays, since so many interactions are virtual, I encourage sidebar moments before or after the event that are more about self-disclosure and sharing. Good team leaders managing virtually understand and include this time as being critical to team identity and employee engagement. In my coaching, I've suggested working the thought distortion model on professional networking activities so they can reframe how they think about it. It is an opportunity to make a meaningful connection rather than a phony, opportunistic interaction.

Enter any networking activity with a spirit of curiosity. Take time to clarify the value you bring to these interactions rather than what you need from people. If there is someone you are planning to meet, look them up on Google, LinkedIn, or Facebook, taking note of anything you might have in common or that you are legitimately curious about. Curiosity has been the key to entering into all kinds of interactions with other global health professionals. Let your curiosity, not a list of memorized questions, drive you in making a good impression. The mind shift is less about you and more about the other person.

Networking gold is not just one-time interactions but contact over time. Keep connected via social media or, best of all, send connections information that would be helpful to them based on your knowledge of them, their needs, and interests. Further, be real. Be honest about who you are. At a conference cocktail event, even expressing your discomfort with the whole networking thing can be a way of clearing the air and getting down to authentically connecting with another person.

A special note to introverts who dislike small talk. If you are curious whether you qualify as an introvert, think about how much you dislike talking with a chatty airplane seatmate or a taxi driver. One solution to this discomfort is to volunteer for a role at a conference—checking people in, being on the info desk—or better yet, sign up to be a presenter or speaker. Let them come to you. Another option is not to do this entirely alone. Bring a friend or colleague. Preferably, it should be someone who knows your accomplishments or who likely knows others in the room so you can trade "warm introductions." Just make sure you're having conversations with other attendees, not just the friends you brought with you.

The opening line is probably one of the most complex parts for an introvert. Have a few opening lines ready. Questions don't have to be profound, just ones that can kickstart a conversation. Classic introductions include, "What are some things you are doing right now that you are excited about?" and "How do you spend most of your time?" "What's your favorite country to work in?" "What brought you to this conference/meeting?" I have found being alone at these events has worked well. I walk up to a small group that doesn't appear to be in an "intense" conversation, introduce myself, and ask something general about the event, such as what they thought of the speaker's content. Leading with curiosity often results in asking them questions about themselves or whether they know other speakers or colleagues.

The topic of professional networking can aid personal exploration of where you might fall in the extraversion-introversion range. The Myers-Briggs Type Indicator (www.themyersbriggs.com) and the Enneagram Test (www.enneagramworldwide.com) are globally validated approaches based on a theory by psychoanalyst Carl Jung. Jung saw extraversion and introversion as two different attitudes or tendencies that affect people's attention in any situation and how they draw conclusions about what they perceive. MBTI and the Enneagram have tools people can use to uncover a set of preferences. They are both complex systems that apply to professional networking. In the MBTI instrument, your preference for extraversion and introversion affects choices regarding your direct perception of judgment, mainly on the outer world (extroversion, E) or the world of ideas (introversion, I). Does being with other people energize you or exhaust you? Is your alone time vital to recovery or a critical recharging time? The E-I preference is a range, so a person can have both E and I tendencies, but how you describe yourself will influence the strategy you choose to develop and maintain your professional network.

Another great model to explore is the Enneagram. The spiritual philosopher George Gurdjieff introduced the Enneagram personality typing system to the modern world around 1915, though its roots are much older. The word "Enneagram" stems from the Greek words *enea*, meaning "nine," and *gramma*, meaning "written" or "drawn." This model uses a circular diagram of nine points that reflect nine different ways of seeing the world. Although they are all connected, each of us has a specific perspective that dominates. It is an excellent tool for self-discovery. Several good books have been written by my mentor, Dr. David Daniels, a psychiatrist who brought the Enneagram to Stanford Medical School and the Stanford Business School. His book *The Essential Enneagram* is a great primer. Another great mentor was Helen Palmer, who taught the Enneagram worldwide. Both have written extensively. Helen Palmer's book *The Enneagram in Love and Work* was a brilliant exposition of how the nine types interact in one's professional and personal life. I bring these tools up now because how you connect with others will make a difference regarding the quality and resilience of your professional network. Plus, it is an excellent opportunity to strengthen your inner observer, and support your personal growth.

Whether you are an extrovert, introvert, or in between, there is a networking strategy that will work for you. The more you are planful and strategic, the more efficient, effective, and successful your professional networking will be.

Explore both internal and external networking opportunities. Don't neglect networking opportunities within your organization. Some workplaces foster more "random collisions"—unexpected interactions that some experts think are a key to creativity. There are also working groups, some of which are voluntary, that often include staff outside of your immediate team. Working on projects outside your department presents invaluable opportunities to deepen the bench strength of your professional network. One of the positive outcomes of working virtually (besides no commuting time and being in your pajama bottoms during meetings) has been widening professional networks beyond the standard in-person office configuration. Fast Company suggests that "if you've always wanted to build a relationship with someone in another department, take advantage of the fact that everyone is working remotely to reach out and suggest a call or video meeting." It is much easier to send an introductory email than it is to initiate a first in-person encounter.

Identify industry conferences, seminars, workshops, and networking events that align with your professional interests. There are any number of large convenings in the field of global health, and then there are technical-specific or population-specific conferences. Many of these events are virtual or hybrid, and they often feature small group breakouts during virtual events that foster connections. New conveners are organizing new events on new topics all the time, so it is up to you to use your knowledge management competency to keep abreast of interesting opportunities. If you're not sure where to start, ask your network! Convenings happen worldwide, so seek out those that meet your needs. I tend to go to CUGH, Global Health Council, USAID, WHO/UN events, Devex, Gallup, CSIS events, and the many convenings in the Washington, DC, area where I am located. Participate actively in these gatherings, engage in conversations, and exchange contact information with individuals who share common interests, feel simpatico, or can contribute to your goals. If you've attended once, consider presenting the next time—on a panel or a workshop or sharing your work. Most large conferences outline processes on their websites, and decisions are made well before the event. Join professional associations and groups and participate in industry-specific organizations, associations, or communities. Attend their events, join committees, or volunteer for leadership roles. These groups provide opportunities to connect with like-minded professionals and can help you establish yourself as an active participant in your field.

Follow up and maintain relationships. After meeting someone, follow up with a personal message to express your gratitude and reinforce the connection. Stay in touch by periodically reaching out, sharing relevant articles or resources, or meeting for coffee. Building and maintaining relationships requires ongoing effort.

Leverage online platforms. In previous chapters, we've discussed using platforms like LinkedIn to get your story out there and make yourself accessible to recruiters. Professional networking platforms can also expand your reach and connect with industry professionals. Use the advice in chapter 7 to build a compelling profile that showcases your skills and experience, and then post content and engage with others. Consider joining relevant online groups, participating in discussions to establish your presence, and messaging those who interest you. Not everyone on social media may be considered a personal connection, but you can still seek advice and ideas from the groups connected to you. You can also use LinkedIn to view the profiles of people before you meet with them. View the profiles from a position of honest curiosity, and you will likely come up with meaningful questions for you and the person you plan to contact.

Seek introductions and referrals. If you are in active job-hunting mode, feel free to ask your existing contacts for introductions to people they know who can help you in your professional journey. Referrals from trusted individuals can open doors and provide you with valuable opportunities. Your professional contacts can help you expand your network and advise about organizations you are interested in, people you would like to meet, and job vacancies for which you might be a good fit. This part of job hunting is often a series of linkages—someone gives you a name or two, and then those give others' names. It helps if you can be specific about your "ask." If someone is willing to send an introductory email to connect both of you, it is a great favor, but don't assume everyone has the time to do it.

Offer value. Networking is not just about asking for favors. Look for ways to add value to your connections. Share industry insights, provide recommendations, and help or connect people who could benefit from knowing each other. By offering your assistance, you establish yourself as a valuable resource. Give before you receive. Show your willingness to help others without expecting an immediate return. Offer your assistance, share your knowledge, and provide support when you can. Being generous and genuine in your interactions will enhance your reputation and foster stronger connections. If you worked in an organization or for people who operated from a "knowledge is power" mentality and liked to hoard information without sharing, now is the time to let that thinking go. The more generous you are, the more information will come back to you.

Develop and value mentors. When considering your network, don't neglect your mentors, as they can be the most valuable part of your professional network. Not every teacher is a mentor. A mentor is an experienced and trusted advisor who provides guidance, support, and knowledge to you, the object of this abundance of gifts. A mentor is a role model who shares their expertise, insights, and experiences to help you navigate challenges, develop skills, and achieve your personal and professional goals. The mentor–mentee relationship in your professional network is typically characterized by trust, mutual respect, and a commitment to your growth and development. Mentors offer guidance, feedback, encouragement, and sometimes even open doors to new opportunities. They provide wisdom, motivation, and support, helping you gain confidence, make informed decisions, and reach your potential. Mentors are not just for early career professionals; they are valuable at every career stage. Finding a mentor is a process, and it may take time to see the right fit. Many of these relationships happen organically in school or on the job. Some organizations have formal mentoring programs, so if you are clear about your goals, they can match you with someone who would meet your needs. Also, that person you admire might have indicated they are available for the role. Stay persistent, be open to opportunities, and continue to seek guidance from various sources throughout your professional journey. Some key steps to help you in the mentoring process are as follows.

1. Be clear about your goals. Think about what you want from the mentor relationship. What would you like to know or be able to do because of their advice, guidance, and support? What do you hope to gain from a mentoring relationship? This

clarity will help you identify the type of mentor you need and help them understand your needs.

2. Define your ideal mentor. Consider the qualities, skills, and experiences you seek in a mentor. Think about individuals who have succeeded in your desired field or possess expertise in areas you want to develop. Qualities should include personal characteristics that would allow you to trust that individual.

3. Network and seek referrals. Engage your online and offline professional network to connect with potential mentors. Seek referrals from colleagues, professors, or industry professionals who may know someone suitable for a conversation about the topic, problem, or situation you'd like to address.

4. Reach out with purpose. Once you've identified potential mentors, approach them with a clear and concise message explaining why you admire their work and believe they would be valuable mentors. Demonstrate your enthusiasm and commitment to your goals, and articulate what is in it for them if they invest time in you.

5. Build rapport. When you connect with a potential mentor, focus on building a genuine relationship. Show interest in their experiences and seek their advice on your challenges. Respect their time and establish an agreed-upon schedule for meetings or communication.

6. Be receptive and open-minded. Mentors can provide valuable insights and feedback if you are open to receiving constructive criticism and advice, even if it challenges your current perspective. Demonstrating a willingness to learn and grow will enhance the mentoring relationship.

7. Take initiative. A mentor's role is to guide and support you, but you must take ownership of your growth. Be proactive in seeking advice, asking questions, and pursuing opportunities.

Show that you value their guidance by applying their advice to your professional development.

8. Maintain regular communication. Keep the lines of communication open and maintain appropriate contact with your mentor. Update them on your progress, seek guidance when needed, and share your successes and challenges. Be sure to show your appreciation for their time and support. Their time is valuable, so be efficient in how much you take.

9. Foster a two-way relationship. Remember that mentoring is a reciprocal process. Offer your skills, knowledge, or assistance to your mentor whenever possible. By providing value in return, you strengthen the mentorship bond and create a mutually beneficial relationship. As a mentor, I appreciated the technology expertise my mentees offered; their assistance was invaluable.

10. Express gratitude. Acknowledge and express gratitude for your mentor's guidance, advice, and support. Let them know how their involvement has positively affected your personal and professional growth. If they are on LinkedIn, endorse them. Make your appreciation public if you think they would find it valuable.

Be patient and persistent. Building a solid professional network takes time. Be consistent in your efforts. Start in your early years and track your network in your phone contacts or spreadsheets, noting technical areas and how you know them. Some connections take time to develop, and opportunities may arise unexpectedly. Remember that the keys are communicating clearly, establishing relationships, and giving back or adding value. Networking is a long-term investment in your professional growth. Focus on building meaningful relationships, adding value, and fostering a strong network of trusted connections.

CHAPTER 11

Interacting with Potential Employers and Coworkers

- What is the informational interview, and how can I ace it?
- What are the best practices regarding the pre-interview, the interview, and post-interview communications?
- What are some considerations when deciding if the position is the right fit and negotiating the entire package?

In this chapter, I focus on all the activities you would implement in a job search, focusing on critical moments of interaction—on the phone, in writing, and in person. Because so much of international development is done in teams and alliances, the work is generally not a solo situation. Your skills in interacting with others are critical during the job-hunting process. As soon as you are at the table during any meet and greet, you are assessing them, and they are assessing you, and the question everyone is asking is, "How does this person fit on my team or in my company?" It would be best if you were asking the same thing. "Would I enjoy working with these people?" So, let's focus on the interpersonal interactions reflected in the informational interview, the pre-interview interactions, the in-person or virtual interview(s), and the post-interview communications with others, both written and oral. I've also included in this chapter the negotiations that commence once your potential employer has signaled that they are interested in you. Separate from professional networking, these are interactions that pertain to seeking and obtaining employment that involve other people and call upon a skillful way of communicating. Your interpersonal skills and tools in this territory contribute significantly to your selection. So, let's start with the informational interview.

Informational Interviewing

In many industries, it is not uncommon for senior professionals to set aside time to meet with people who are interested in learning more about their industry, organization, work, and personal career path. Meeting seekers don't necessarily need to be job hunters, so informational interviews can also be a tool in your "professional networking" arsenal.

Most who seek informational interviews fall into these categories: early career, industry switchers, job hunters, and anyone who wants to learn about something that they think this person knows about—their job, their company, their technical areas, a particular country, and the like. In my earlier global health days, I was fortunate to meet people who had written the books everyone was using or talking about. I took advantage of engaging in deeper conversations than most, which they probably didn't expect. I was a midcareer professional making an industry switch, so I had a steep learning curve. I purchased a *New York Times* bestseller, *Getting Things Done* by David Allen, at an airport. The content blew me away, so I called his company and asked to speak with him. That conversation turned into his becoming a consultant to my project, which resulted in workflow management habits that I, and many others in global health, still use twenty years later. Now, I also have hit brick walls with people's assistants, so I used informal meeting occasions—the only decent reason to go to a cocktail party besides seeing friends—to connect and request a meeting later.

Keep track of authors you like, researchers and public speakers you respect, people in various positions of authority who seem to either have the kind of job that you want or are embedded in the company where you might like to work, or people you come across who are doing things that interest you. These are often busy professionals who only have a certain amount of time to give to someone they do not know or do not need anything from. So, consider what the value of talking with you is to them. One of the great things about this industry is that we can easily remember when we were knocking on people's doors, trying to understand the path forward, or learning from those who have gone before. There is an emphasis on senior leaders being mentors to others, sharing information, and even figuring out the below-awareness tacit knowledge. Most will be gracious and consider informational interviews an aspect of their professional lives. But a word of caution: an informational interview differs from a mentoring relationship. Mentoring relationships are commitments over time when someone sincerely advises and supports your entire professional movement forward. I have had people come to me and ask if I would be their mentor. I have learned to say a polite no, give them other ideas about establishing that relationship, and encourage them to develop those ties organically with people who already know them. I've also reflected on how frustrating it is to feel that there isn't anyone on your side to help you.

In your informational interview, lead with honest curiosity and respect for their time. If you hear someone speak or are introduced to someone of interest to you, politely ask in a general way if you might take fifteen to thirty minutes or so to seek their knowledge on a particular topic. Do your homework about the person, the company, and the industry. Come prepared with interesting questions, and take at most thirty minutes of their time. Of course, if they offer to spend more time in the meeting, consider that a good sign and continue.

And now for a dark moment. If an informational interview feels inappropriate or "off," trust your intuition and politely depart immediately. It's not your job to make everything sound ok or soothe their ruffled feathers. Predators, unfortunately, can show up anywhere, and there have been plenty of scandals to prove it. The experienced ones make you feel you have misunderstood them or are to blame and should be ashamed for "wasting my time." It's hard to believe, but some consider the power differential an opportunity to behave horrendously. It's disheartening and enraging at the same time. Just be smart and stick with your professional boundaries to protect your spirit. Don't keep this story a secret. Immediately share your experience with a trusted friend or colleague. Having run fellowship and internship programs and worked internationally, I've had more than one job seeker or young employee in my office in tears. With their permission, I was pleased to out these sometimes-revered senior people. You may choose to do nothing about it, but acknowledging that it happened, that the person is a creep, and that you did nothing wrong sometimes lessens any residue of shame and secrecy.

Let's assume this never happens to you, and this person is as wise and helpful as you hoped they would be. In informational interviews, your goal is to make a connection and learn something useful, so come to the virtual or in-person moment with questions whose answers will aid you. Some ideas to get you thinking would be questions like, What made you decide to work here? What do you love most about working in this job? In this organization? In this industry? I've read about your work, but could you tell me more about your professional history? How did you get from where you were to where you are now? What do you think it takes to be successful here? What's some advice you wish you had been given before you started working here or in global health? When you were my age, what did you wish someone had told you?

The informational interview will improve if you mute any thirst for a job. Take a moment and let your curiosity come to the fore. Think about the person you're talking to as a human being with a deep history and many hard-won lessons. Communicate a value that you have on their time and their wisdom.

Telephone or Virtual Pre-Interview

When it comes to interviewing for a new position, if someone from the company calls you, you have moved from the decarded résumé pile into the "we're curious" pile. Congratulations! The pre-interview means your résumé has been accepted, and the hiring manager is interested in learning more about you. Perhaps there is something about your résumé and cover letter that requires clarification. Maybe your written materials sparked some curiosity, and they need to get more information or more of an impression of you as an employee. It could be that your professional networking and informational interviews bore fruit, and you were preselected because of a personal connection with the company or hiring manager. Or, if you are an internal candidate, protocol requires that you automatically be considered at this stage.

The pre-interview contact is typically done not by the final decision-maker(s) but by the human resources office staff or a member of your potential final team. Sometimes, it is a professional recruitment company that prescreens you before advancing your résumé. In any case, they've read your résumé and cover letter. This is when they ask you questions to clarify dates or fill in some gaps. Make no mistake: this is when your interpersonal competence is in play for the first time. This first contact begins their assessment of your interpersonal style. Before the interview begins, take a deep breath, speak with a smile even if they can't see you, and trust that all your preparation makes you sufficient for the task. It may help to remember that not only are they hiring you, but you are also hiring them. You are deciding whether to choose them as your employer. You are not powerless.

Suppose you are sweating bullets because you've fudged some of the information, overblown it, or maybe didn't finish that degree. Well, learn your lesson, fix it, and never do it again. Companies will work to confirm the information you've provided, and finding an anomaly is a dealbreaker for almost all organizations. Reference checks are required for most positions now. I've seen people hired and start working only to soon get fired because they were a semester away from the MPH, but their résumé indicated it was earned. Many companies now do background checks for histories with police as well as any legal actions and credit reports. If you are seeking a position in the federal government, there may be other considerations, such as meeting security clearance requirements.

But mostly, what's happening in this pre-interview is a check of your interpersonal skills. If you've done it correctly, the résumé has given them all the essential information but has not fleshed you out as a human being. Human resource offices often ask for a pre-interview to determine whether you are a good fit for the group you will be joining. Display any interpersonal skills necessary for the position. Be professional, but let your personality show. If you believe you are a go-getter, energetic, wise, and a good listener, now is an excellent time to show those qualities. There are two decisions that I always suggest to my clients when they are preparing for these pre-interviews. Choose to be curious, and choose to be confident. Display your essential emotional intelligence and personal security. Oh, you haven't worked on these? Now's the time. Confidence is not pride or arrogance but is impactful when balanced with appropriate, authentic self-knowledge. It's also important not to overstate your experience and skills. As in résumé development, don't believe everything you've heard about using grandiose adjectives. Please don't do it when describing yourself, either. I've seen and heard "transformational leader" so many times that it has lost meaning.

The pre-interview is a mini practice for the job interview, so don't be afraid to ask a few questions about which you might be curious. They'll tell you immediately if they know enough to provide that information. There is a better time to make demands, negotiate salary benefits, and more. But read the package negotiation section of this chapter before you have first contact with your potential employers. Finally, always ask about the next steps and send a short thank-you note to the person who called you. If there is anything you particularly appreciate about the interaction, let them know. Everyone enjoys authentic positive comments.

Knowing What's Important to You

Every chapter of this book requires you to act or do some personal work. The outcome is that you are more ready than most to focus on key considerations when job hunting. Consider making this a checklist with personal notes regarding your preferences. These include the location, job title and responsibilities, company history and values, benefits, salary, work hours, workplace culture and environment, work-life balance, and workplace flexibility such as virtual/in-person/hybrid work, professional development and advancement, employee appreciation and recognition, the team and management, tools and technology, and communication.

The Job Interview

When you are asked to come in for a job interview or a virtual meeting, take a moment to smile, dance, or relish the recognition that you are part of a select group under consideration. Much of the advice I've presented for the pre-interview also applies to the job interview. In many organizations, you've graduated from an applicant to a candidate. Fantastic! You've probably done your homework on the organization and perhaps talked with a company employee. A question like, "What do you wish someone had told you when you first started here?" is good to ask. You've thoroughly reviewed the job description, including circling and highlighting your best guess about the keywords, top priority skills, and experience, and compared your résumé to the keywords. Perhaps you've run the job description through an AI program, asking for crucial qualities. You've probably gathered many "typical interview questions" over the Internet, so you may have already worked yourself into a panic. Not yet? Great! The next step is preparation.

You may only meet with one person or be invited to a series of meetings with different people who will provide feedback about you and may have differing powers of influence over the hiring decision. More typical is a panel, either virtually or in person. Human resource offices have become sensitive to potential litigation in the hiring process. As protection, they often interview in groups and decide beforehand on a set of required questions for all candidates and a scoring sheet used for all candidates that typically reflects the keywords in the position description. So, whether the interview is an individual or a panel, there is usually a set of questions they will ask every candidate. They compare answers, score interviews, and create consensus. Often, companies request those score sheets be kept on file in case of a discrimination lawsuit. But that doesn't mean that the follow-up or secondary questions won't be based on something you've shared or a personal interest you've sparked.

The job interview will likely cover some expected and familiar territory. I've grouped typical questions into general categories you should consider. The most important thing is keeping in mind the value you bring to the organization. Most job interviews will include one or more of the following elements.

Icebreakers

Formal interviews can be nerve-wracking and challenging for candidates. Remember, be curious and confident. You've got this. You've done your homework and have an answer for any question that might come up. Don't forget that you are also choosing whether you want to work for them while they are deciding whether you are a good fit for the position. Notice their efforts to welcome you—to break the ice. Respond to a "tell us about yourself" with your elevator speech that you have practiced in the past. Keep it short. Do they initiate small talk that helps to make you feel welcome? Or is the initial interaction designed to make you uncomfortable somehow? These "tests" don't bode well for company culture, and the organizational culture matching your values is a critical factor in where you work. It directly contributes to your job satisfaction and your performance.

Match Your Skills and Experience with What's Required in the Job

When thinking about this position, what are the top three to four skills that would make you good at this job? You've dissected the job description and your résumé, so have a few concise stories that reflect the match. Describe what you have done and how it turned out. This is an excellent time to do a PSR: What was the problem? What was the solution? What were the results or outcomes? When you use metrics that quantify your success, hiring managers are more likely to remember your contributions. I've noticed that these are the things that interviewers write down during interviews.

Self-Reflection and Self-Disclosure: Your Greatest Accomplishments and Most Significant Failures

Typically, these are the mistakes you've made on the job or successes you have had. Interviewers may also want to know how you define success in your current role. Prepare and practice different ways of answering until the message feels "right" to you, that is, authentic. Remember, you want to be hired, so this is no time to be so brutally honest that they fear you. There is no reason to scare anyone with too much self-disclosure. They will want to hear about difficult situations you've encountered at work and how you overcame them. Think ahead on this topic so that your answers are authentic and valid. This is the beginning of the trusting relationship you want with your employer. They have heard "I work too hard," "I'm a perfectionist," "I give my all," and "I'm a workaholic" many times. And if that is your exact answer, go with that, but dig deeper as well. This preparation is another example of how your awake inner observer can serve you. Above all, however, any failures you share should always be accompanied by lessons learned.

Working in Groups, Collaborating on Teams, and Workforce Conflict

Global health work is usually done through international alliances, diverse working groups, and multicultural teams, so think this through and craft stories that reflect your strengths. Illustrate your interpersonal competence through your stories and how you tell them. If this is a panel interview, your interpersonal skills will be on display in the meeting, so be sure to back up your examples of being a good, respectful listener and collaborator with matching behaviors during the interview. In chapter 7, we explored the role of the résumé, which cannot communicate your soft skills effectively. From the first contact with the organization, you are being evaluated regarding your interpersonal skills. They may request examples, so they have a few stories on hand, but you may be presented with hypothetical scenarios and asked what you would do. There are many ways to get this right, so be your authentic self—that wise, self-aware person who can communicate your preferences and strengths in working with others.

If you are an internal candidate, the interview will go into more depth. Again, having an example of a PSR would be helpful. You should also be ready to answer questions about how this department, team, or position relates to other positions and internal and external stakeholders, partners, and donors. If your evaluation scores are generally high, you can share a few evaluation results as an example of how others have historically perceived your work. If previous employers have used 360-degree reports and you have rated well, include something related to this metric. A 360-degree report is a performance evaluation assessment tool using feedback from peers, subordinates, supervisors, and sometimes external stakeholders to provide a more holistic view of an individual's performance. If you have organized your files according to the guidance in chapter 7, your evaluation data will be readily available, aiding you in preparing for the interviews.

Innovation and Creativity

It is now more common to test your creativity by asking how you might improve on something, or you could be asked to come up with outside-the-box solutions to hypothetical problems. They might ask you to detail two or three steps you would take to make a difference in the organization. First and most important, take a few deep breaths. Then, let your mind flow. Part of your pre-interview preparation was reading this book chapter and thinking about a few common issues in your technical area. Now is the time to share your thoughts, taking care to respect different points of view or other strategies.

You may be asked how you would reconcile opposing dynamics or goals within the organization and or negotiate competing pressures within the company. Questions about what makes the position attractive or what skills you hope to develop in this new position may also come up.

Problem Solving

When it comes to sharing your approach to solving problems, interviewers may pose scenarios but also ask you to discuss examples from your professional experience. Here again the PSR technique is helpful (see the résumé section in chap. 7), whereby you share the problem you faced, how you solved it, and what happened because of the solution. Embedded in this question might be something about your pet peeves. This is your opportunity to share what bothers you, but you should be mindful to include your strategies for addressing the things that bug you. This territory may also comprise a question about why you want to leave your current position.

Managing Interpersonal Conflict, Promoting Collaboration

You may also be asked to identify a professional interpersonal situation where you disagreed with a colleague, how the conflict was resolved, and what you learned from it. How do you promote collaboration and teamwork within and across organizational boundaries? They would like you to give them an example and tell them the outcome. They'll be looking at how you handle interpersonal conflict and how you see yourself as a collaborator or team member. That doesn't shut the door on the fact that you can come in with your own plans for the organization, but they want to ensure you have a deeper understanding of an issue's history, the case's context, and the needs of everyone involved. It's an opportunity for you to share your wisdom and your ability to collaborate.

Management Skills and Supervisory Know-How

If you are interviewing for a supervisory or management position, hiring managers will want to know how you interact with both superiors and direct reports. Sometimes, this territory will show up as a question, asking for a story about a good or bad manager. Be prepared to share examples from your work history.

The more you know about the realities of the position, the better your interview will be. It gets complicated if an interview panel already knows you, but try not to let that throw you. When you are talking about innovation or changes or fixes, be aware that there might be people on the interview panel who were the ones who created those changes or caused those situations. Take care to preface your remarks with statements such as, "Others' perspectives and needs deeply influence all of this, but I do have some thoughts about it" or "I would want to enter the position and gain a better understanding from those around me of what forces created the situation and what has already been done to try to address it." Make it clear that your initial thoughts in this job interview might shift once you learn more about the context of the problem.

Do You Have Any Questions for Us?

Just a few points here. The job interview isn't the time to ask about salary, benefits, or paid time off. You should do your homework before the interview, so don't ask any questions about the company that you couldn't answer yourself by checking out its website. Don't ask what they are looking for in the position, and don't say you don't have any questions! Appropriate questions to ask interviewers include those about the company values, how they might describe the organization's culture, how long they've been with the company, and what they like about working there. These are topics that invite them to self-disclose in positive ways. It's always a good idea to ask about next steps and timing of the hiring process. Finally, you should thank them for their time and compliment them for the quality of the questions they asked.

To reiterate, the most common mistakes you can make in an interview are arriving late, being inappropriately dressed, answering your phone during the interview, talking badly about any former company or employer, talking so much that interviewers can't get their questions in, not asking questions yourself, being unprepared, not telling the truth, or being inattentive. Finally, answer and ask all questions with enthusiasm and a smile.

One of the most common reasons people leave their jobs is because they do not like their bosses. If your future manager is a panel member or the sole interviewer, be aware of how that person presents themselves to you. And think seriously about what it would be like to work for them. Remember that you are being interviewed for the position and are also in the process of considering them as an employer. You have the right to decide if this is a good fit. Other red flags include: (1) a disorganized hiring process, which could be a reflection of the company's daily operations; (2) a salary range that is below the market rate, what was advertised, or what you might have discussed or expected; (3) a position that sounds like a dead-end with no advancement opportunities; (4) interviewers that are tight-lipped, avoiding eye contact, or barely responding; (5) there is a lengthy provisional/probationary/trial period, which may mean fewer benefits and less job security; and (6) it just does not feel right. Pay attention to these red flags. As a reader of this book, you are informed with analytical skills and an activated intuition, the awake inner observer.

When you have your list of most likely areas to be explored in the interview, consider writing down some answers. Then, putting yourself in that desired role, write a response. Have a friend ask you questions and listen as if they were the interviewer. Practice the discussion and practice answering the questions out loud. You can keep paper on hand to take notes during the interview, a comforting and feasible tool especially when an interview is virtual. I call this my "cheat sheet."

I recently helped someone with a senior position in a well-known international organization prepare for a job interview within his organization. He came to me because he felt paralyzed after a previous "failed" interview and was beginning to think thoughts like "I am a terrible interviewee" or "I will always panic during interviews." These thought distortions didn't serve him well and set him up for interview failure. The norm in his organization was to hire internal candidates, if possible. He came to me for coaching because he was now seriously paralyzed by his negative thoughts. He was beginning to believe that he would never get a better position. He told me he was concerned that his career was over and that he had topped out. I pushed for some analysis of these thought distortions while suggesting that he analyze the interview that did not lead to his selection. He had secretly taped the interview on his cellphone, so we had all the questions. (I'm pretty sure this was illegal, so I'm not recommending you record your interviews, but the analysis of the recording benefited this exercise.) We organized the questions into the typical categories of interview questions, and he rethought his answers, exploring why he would answer that way. When a second job came open (which was an even better fit), he took those questions and wrote the kinds of responses he wished he had said, and then we practiced several times until he felt polished and calm. One strategy was to address his resting/thinking expression—frowning, eyes cast downward, mouth turned down—which conveyed an unfriendly or angry affect, though that was not how he felt inside. Nor was it his intent. So, on his cheat sheet, he drew smiley faces and eyeballs to remind him to look at the interviewers and to smile at them. The other trick that helped lead to the interview's success was to compliment the interviewer on how good the question was when he needed a moment to think about a response. You can't use this technique frequently, but if you do it a few times, it can be charming because those interviewers want to be good. This is a performance moment for themselves as well as you, one that leaves a positive impression.

The final tip for the interview process is to help with the meeting flow. Suppose you are a person who tends to run on and speak too long. In that case, it sometimes can be frustrating to the interviewer(s), who may have a list of questions they are required to ask all candidates. So, when you are finished with a question, say something like, "Turning it back to you," or nodding as a signal that you have finished speaking. Do not feel that you need to fill every pause with conversation. If they need more information, they will ask for it. Or they may ask a follow-up question.

The job interview is a high-stakes moment for any job seeker. You have no natural way of understanding all the subtext and context that influence how your answers land on the ears of the panel or the interviewer, so you might as well relax and settle into a few honest statements. Find a way to ask questions of your own with enthusiasm and a smile.

You may have multiple callbacks or a request to speak with others. Getting feedback on the first interview and what the hiring managers are looking for is helpful. Ask questions like, "What would help you make this decision?" Or "What areas would you like more information from me on?" Their answers will help you prepare to go deeper or in a different direction in your follow-up interviews.

If you have the opportunity, you can request to speak with potential colleagues. Below is a list of a few questions to which the answers might be helpful to you.

- What made you decide to work here?
- What do you love most about working here?
- How does one become successful here?
- What's some advice you wish you had been given before you started working here?
- What do you wish you knew back when you took the job versus now?
- How would you describe the organizational culture?
- If you could change one thing in the organization, what would it be?

After the Interview

The day after your interview, send everyone you spoke with an email sincerely thanking them for the time they gave you, noting how helpful it was to learn more about the company and the position, and reiterating that you are more interested than ever in working there. Let them know you would be happy to provide additional information if that would support them moving forward with their decision. Be patient. Human resource systems are notorious for taking longer than they even project to make these decisions. Often, this has nothing to do with you and your candidacy.

After the Job Offer

If you're at the end of the interview and the employer is interested in you, you might get a job offer then and there. Only accept a job offer once you've done your homework on the organization. Revisit what is important to you, keeping focused on your priorities.

With all the additional information you gained during the interview, recheck the company website to confirm your feelings for the organization's work and culture; even if the website text is aspirational, it still matters. Many organizations now provide information on the benefits and salary ranges for positions when they advertise the vacancy. For nonprofits, consider checking out www.guidepost.com to access their 990 IRS form, which gives the salaries of their top highest-earning staff. It may not be comparable to your salary, but it may give you some negotiating leverage if you are a senior staffer. Sites like Glassdoor and Comparably share research and anonymous reviews of many companies. You want to work for companies with a 3.5-star rating or higher.

Negotiating the Compensation Package

For any employment offer, consider the entire compensation and experience package, not just the salary. How important are working virtually, paid maternity/paternity leave, tuition reimbursement, retirement contributions, paid parking or public transportation, paid time off, work-at-home policies, time spent traveling, business- or economy-class seating, professional development time, and funding support? Are there bonuses, workshare, and buybacks? What are the retirement benefits? What are the health benefits for an individual or a family, whatever your circumstances? Is there a suitable travel allowance? What must you do if working virtually or at home is essential, and does the organization provide equipment and support in your home office? If your basic living needs can be met, you can negotiate different terms to make the package attractive, even if the salary differs from what you hoped for. You can include in the conversation all kinds of perks, bonuses, and potential evaluation/salary increases before or at the one-year mark. Consider professional development funds and retirement account additions. For example, the Public Health Institute (PHI) added 10 percent of my salary as a contribution to my retirement every year. It was also beneficial when they combined vacation and sick days into one bank of PTO (paid time off). When I resigned from PHI, I received all the PTO days I had not used in one lump sum. When I worked at Johns Hopkins University, there was significant tuition remission for the children of employees.

Think holistically. You will know some of this information if you've done your investigative work well. How does this position fit with the vision that you created during the earlier parts of this book? How many compromises would you need to make, or does this work ultimately support your vision?

Thinking of yourself as a business of one, what compromises will you make? Will this position set you up for the next job, and the job after that? How much of your vision are you willing to let go of, for now? And what are your must-haves? For some, it is the travel time—either limiting it or traveling as much as possible. For others, it might be being present in the office versus working at home. What's important to you is an impressive list, which will change with each job because your life will change. Think ahead before you go into the negotiation.

The salary conversation is among the most challenging aspects of seeking a new position. You can price yourself out of contention, undervalue what you bring, or settle for something that forces you to get a second job or continue to seek other employment. Leaving unexpectedly and early is unsuitable for your résumé, potential references, and reputation. Do not accept a deal that will leave you going to work every day feeling resentful and mistreated. Those feelings will leak out, and you could become the problem employee. In my first job after graduate school, I accepted the salary I was offered and didn't realize until shortly after I arrived that I was working alongside men with BAs earning more than me. I pointed this out and renegotiated within the first three months but never trusted my supervisor again.

The goal in salary negotiations is for both the employer and the employee to feel good about the agreement, and there is usually a middle ground that works for both. It helps to research the company and compare what you find to your needs and vision. The good news is that there are plenty of things that you can do before the conversation to prepare you for the position, determining a salary range that reflects your needs and your value.

When it comes to salary, know your bottom line and be prepared to walk away if the offer can't match it. The walk-away wage is the least amount you and yours need to live. When you're thinking about the salary question, start with your budget. What amount do you need to live the life you want? The answer to this question is not the "I've won the lottery" fantasy life, but getting your needs met, including saving for retirement as well as fun and joy now. If you have not determined your necessary income, now is the time to create a budget, including all monthly and recurring expenses such as car and health insurance, car repair, school fees, annual taxes, vacations, and so on. Several promising programs are out there to help you create and monitor your budget. My go-to is ynab.com (YNAB stands for You Need a Budget). If you are early career, check out the books *Financial Feminist* (for all genders) or *Rich AF* to get a good starting handle on investing and saving. If you are seeking employment in another city or country, take your budget and translate those expenses into the cost of living for that environment. Real estate websites and other Internet searches will help you with this exercise. You don't want to have a bottom-line amount for Wichita when moving to Los Angeles or living in Bangkok, Nairobi, or Washington, DC.

When you have your bottom-line number, ask yourself, "Will I be satisfied with this salary?" A 2023 survey from a financial services company, Empower, asked two thousand people exactly how much money they think they need to be happy. People with a median salary of $65,000 said a median of $95,000, while those with a median of $250,000 gave a median response of $350,000. Nonunion annual raises are expected to be 3.9 percent in 2024, but survey respondents indicated needing 50 percent raises to be happier and less stressed. Most respondents thought having more money would solve most of their problems, but research tells us that people might be happier if they focus on the best ways to use their money rather than getting more of it.

So, be honest about what you are attaching to that number. Are you comparing yourself to others? When I was a child, my father told my mother that he had made $10,000 that year. All I could think of was ten thousand one-dollar bills stacked in a huge pile. For some reason, that became my litmus test for success. You can imagine that thinking that $10,000 was sufficient for an annual salary caused me problems early in my career! So be aware of the baggage that might be linked to specific numbers, and try to free yourself from such expectations so you can realistically analyze how the numbers add up for you.

If you're considering a specific job or are offered a position whose salary is less than what you need to live, you can't afford to accept it. You must continue searching for a job or take a second job. In either case, the situation will be untenable. Do your research before the compensation conversation to understand the fair market value for someone with your experience and the typical salaries for the position you are applying for. As I mentioned previously, today, more companies and organizations publish their salary ranges when they advertise the job, but it still needs to be more common.

It is not so easy to identify an accurate salary range. There are many things that you are going to know if you have inside information. For example, you will need to see the quality and extensiveness of the benefits, the structure, the expenses you may incur related to transportation, and more. Depending on the position you seek, some websites help you uncover the general salary range for various functions. Several websites can help you determine salaries for multiple positions. Some popular ones include:

1. Glassdoor (www.glassdoor.com). Glassdoor provides salary information, company reviews, and interview insights shared by employees. It allows you to search for specific job titles, locations, and companies to understand salary ranges.

2. Salary.com (www.salary.com). Salary.com offers a comprehensive database of salary information for various job titles and industries. It provides salary ranges, bonus information, and other compensation details. It also allows you to customize salary reports based on location and years of experience.

3. PayScale (www.payscale.com). PayScale provides salary data based on job titles, experience, education, and location. It offers a salary calculator that considers various factors to estimate salary ranges for specific positions.

4. Indeed (www.indeed.com/salaries). Indeed, a popular job search engine, provides salary information for different job titles. You can search for salaries by job title, location, and company to understand average wages in your desired field.

5. LinkedIn Salary Insights (www.linkedin.com/salary). LinkedIn Salary Insights provides salary information based on user-submitted data. It allows you to explore salaries by job title, location, industry, and company size. LinkedIn Premium subscribers may have access to more detailed salary data. Getting that information can be expensive, however, so be aware.

6. Comparably (www.comparably.com). Comparably is a newer website with less information, but it is becoming more benefi-

cial as it collects additional data. Besides salaries by position title and zip code, it provides information on the best companies for culture, women, and diversity.

These websites provide general salary estimates and ranges based on aggregated data. Salaries can vary depending on location, company size, industry, experience, and individual negotiation skills. I recommend considering multiple sources and talking with people doing similar work to better understand salary ranges for specific positions.

Create your desired salary range for the specific position you are seeking, and then prepare your comments and questions. Hiring managers or recruiters may ask you about your salary expectations in the first rounds of the interview process. If you can't answer that question, you may appear indifferent, self-doubting, unprepared, and unqualified. So, it's essential to know your value. Consider comments such as "I would be more comfortable with" as opposed to "I want" or "I need." Saying something like "I want to be as flexible as possible" demonstrates your desire to work for the company while sticking up for yourself during salary negotiations. Remind them of the value you bring using the metrics from your résumé. Having a concrete number on the table can relieve some of the tension that can pop up during these types of meetings. Your employer wants to avoid a protracted negotiation. Also, feel free to ask for time to consider their offer, and show appreciation for their help in reaching an agreement.

These interactions with your potential employer, whether the recruiter or the hiring manager, are the beginning of the trust that is so important. Hence your interactions need to be trustworthy. When asked about target salary or range, we often say something vague, like "I'd like to wait and see" or "Let's discuss this later." I've done this myself, thinking I'll wait until I'm their choice and they're committed to me, and then I will have the upper hand. Recruiters often complain about this obvious strategy and do not want to waste their time investigating the fit if you are entirely out of their range. They are buying your service. By having a salary range that you feel comfortable with, you immediately tell them you have a good sense of your value and that you have researched similar positions. It is solid if you can justify your thinking with data. The more research you do, the better you will understand the correct range and the more confident and transparent about your worth you will be. All that information and attitude will help you present and market yourself more effectively to potential employers.

You will stand out in the interview if you are positive, respectful, and transparent about the value you will create for the organization. If they react with surprise to your range, you can always say there are other things to consider; you are open to the conversation if presented with an offer. You will stand out if you present with gratitude, humility, and all the emotional intelligence content we discussed in previous chapters. Be positive, respectful, and polite. I recall hearing stories from my recruitment staff about hiring early career professionals that included belligerent attitudes and unrealistic expectations. I've observed combative candidates who were offered the position but whose rudeness in the negotiation process led to rescinding the offer. Ultimately, the manager didn't want to work with someone with that attitude, even if they were a great technical match.

Sometimes, the highest-salaried new person is the first to be laid off because they are considered to be too expensive. Also, if you take a salary that is too high for the work or where you are career-wise (i.e., it isn't a "fair" wage based on your research), you'll look overpaid. In that case, you will create a new problem: the salary becomes the rate employers expect you to request, and you may be out of sync with the job market for your experience level. Markets always correct themselves as they fluctuate depending on which jobs are most in demand. Be careful not to set yourself up by taking salaries that are too high. Because of automated applicant tracking systems, some companies request the desired salary in the application. Do not leave that blank. If you do, your entire application will likely be tossed out. Sometimes, it's better to put a figure in the midrange. If there is an area in the form for a short response, use it to expand on your history or the needed salary range you will accept.

A tip for LMIC health professionals: the salary differential between the LMIC professional working in your own country versus the HIC organization is substantial. Don't let them use your salary history to pay you less than the going rate for that position for HIC professionals. Many international organizations now use "market rates" to value roles because of the inequity caused by salary histories.

If you receive a surprisingly high-paying offer, ensure you have researched the management and work culture. It is not uncommon for companies that have a hard time retaining employees to start paying more rather than fixing why people are leaving that organization in the first place. Also, in salary negotiations, when you're at that moment when you're talking about your value, don't focus too much on soft skills; focus on your technical skills, your experience, what you know how to do, and its value to the organization.

Once you have received an offer, communicate your gratitude and excitement, but ask for a day or two to consider everything. If you want to negotiate, you could come back to them and say, "I'm wondering if you could meet me at X" with a list of reasons why. At this moment, don't bother with your soft skills. They need the facts on the return on their investment. Because you've done your homework and know something about their culture, you can tell them how you will save them money, enhance their reputation, or get results to back up your value. This is where you make your case. Practice these conversations. Record and listen to your practice presentation even if the research has been done. The more you practice, the more comfortable you will be. Practice it in front of another person, explaining the research you've done and the value you bring. Type up your notes if necessary.

A special note to women: *Lean In: Women, Work, and the Will to Lead*, a book by Sheryl Sandberg, a business executive and the former chief operating officer of Facebook, discusses women's empowerment in the workplace. She describes research on the differences between women and men in the job market. As you might imagine, women struggle the most with the confidence to ask for what they want, need, and deserve. That's why you need to practice these conversations out loud. It may be out of your comfort zone.

Know when to stop or walk away. Think about what might sweeten the deal—an extra week of vacation, more at-home time, a bonus, reconsidering the salary based on performance in six months? If you get two hard no's, the negotiation is probably done. Then you decide. Don't go into a job resenting your new employer, because you'll be looking for another job right away. Another outcome when people take less than what they think they deserve is not feeling connected to their organization.

Perhaps you and your potential new employer can't agree. Keep it positive and respectful, and be grateful for the time they invested in you. Include anyone with whom you made a good connection within your professional network (see chap. 10). Stay in touch with them, because things change in organizations. I know I've been offered positions later with higher rates, and as an employer, I've sought out those who had impressed me previously.

In this chapter, we have explored a transactional aspect of your career strategy. Informational interviews, pre-interview contact, official job interviews, and the various negotiations are all interpersonal behaviors that require preparation, research, and an awake inner observer who is calm, confident, and compassionate toward everyone with whom you interact.

For many, this is career development's most challenging and stressful part. But with the proper preparation, it doesn't have to be so stressful. You got this.

PART IV

BECOMING A LIFELONG CAREER STRATEGIST

CHAPTER 12

Putting It All Together with New Mindsets and Habits

- What is this process in a nutshell?
- What's next?

I wrote this book to provide everything you need to create a global health career strategy that reflects your vision, unique knowledge, attitudes, experience, and skills. I don't care if you are just starting your career or are a world-famous global health rock star. We all must learn how to navigate our professional lives, and all of us occasionally experience internal unhelpful dialogue. I want to change how you think about your professional life so that you are more knowledgeable, on top of things, less stressed, and able take any necessary action. I want you to feel confident, assertive, and in charge, yet peaceful regarding those factors you can't plan for or control. Yes, this takes discipline, especially the courage to face and walk through the ways you diminish your power. I hope you finish this book fully equipped with all the critical know-how to implement an entire career-planning process.

I've broken down all the essential knowledge, attitudes, skills, and experience into chapters that still give you space to fill in the blanks with your unique self. If mastered separately, the work will move you forward dramatically toward the life you can barely imagine. I did this by sorting the content into three components: first, the big picture; second, creating the habits of a lifelong career strategist; and third, the specific transactions and behaviors that are critical aspects of a job search.

Global Health's Big Picture

As detailed in chapters 1–3, start by understanding the global health industry as a researcher, implementer, direct service provider, and businessperson who sees the whole picture. Global health is a multifaceted field that centers on enhancing health and striving for health equity on a global scale. It encompasses various disciplines and addresses all health-related issues, and its business practices are firmly grounded in economic dynamics and relationships among high-income, middle-income, and low-income nations.

I have elevated a particular issue—locally led development or decolonizing global health—because it is essential for GH professionals to have an informed viewpoint. That includes profound shifts in in-country relationships, organizational systems, and various actors' roles in global health. Expect ebbs and flows, surges and reductions as backlash moves the needle. At its core, it's about power sharing, and as a species, our record is not excellent on this subject.

Finally, I want to reinforce that the essential task of strategic career planning shifts throughout every working person's lifetime. Different questions must be addressed throughout your lifespan based on your situation during each period. Graduate school? What kind of graduate school? Overseas experience? What is the right career path for you at this moment? Should you transition from one sector to another? From domestic to global, is the experience different if you are a HIC or LMIC professional? I also emphasize the business-of-one mentality that is key to your career-planning approach. It will help you take a strategic point of view throughout your life and not just at job-hunting time.

In part I, I introduced a subject—competencies—that is familiar to most people in global health because most are graduates of advanced study programs. I used a unique approach to describe the areas of competence you can utilize to determine what is important to you, self-assessing your mastery of four areas: health expertise, the business of global health, interpersonal effectiveness and technology/knowledge management. Take stock of your strengths, skills, and areas of expertise. Identify what you excel at and what you enjoy doing. Notice where you might have gaps or missing content or experience. This self-assessment will help you determine where to thrive and contribute the most. Whether you are looking for graduate programs, your next or last global health position before retirement, or you've already retired and are thinking about focusing only on activities that reflect your gifts and your interests, I want to help you concentrate on those masteries that matter to you and support strategic career moves.

Laying the Foundation for a Lifelong Career Strategy Habit

Chapters 4–7 discuss how to build a foundation through introspection; creating a vision; identifying your knowledge, attitudes, experience, and skills gaps; and then creating and executing a plan to plug those gaps. Through an inquiry of four key questions, I introduced mindful practices to help you access your all-important awake inner observer, bring it up to awareness, analyze it, make conscious decisions about it, and use it however you will.

In part II, key takeaways were using KASE (knowledge, attitudes, skills, and experience) in making strategic career-planning development a lifelong habit, saving you time and stress. I also expanded on attitudes that you might try on the mindset of being the CEO of your corporation, your business of one. It's ok to be open to something better. As your understanding of yourself, skills, and experience evolves, your awareness of your purpose and what is meaningful does, too. You don't have to hate your job or boss to want something else.

Creating a career plan involves envisioning your ideal professional future, which always includes the whole picture of your life. It also means defining the direction and purpose you want to pursue. We explored in this section the various steps to creating a career strategy, including reflecting on your values, interests, and needs for yourself or in partnership with others, starting by understanding what moves you. Consider what activities and subjects you enjoy, what gives you a sense of fulfillment, and what aligns with your core values. Reflecting on these aspects will help you identify the direction you want your career to continue.

Once you envision your ideal professional life, create a road map. Break the big vision into goals and then into smaller, actionable steps. Create a plan that outlines the milestones, skills to acquire, educational requirements, and experiences needed to reach your long-term goals. This plan will provide a structured path and help you stay focused and motivated. Set short- and long-term goals, and develop a goal-getting process. Think about where you see yourself in the long term. What type of work would you like to be doing? What impact would you want to make? Set specific, measurable, achievable, relevant, and time-bound (SMART) goals that align with your vision. These goals will serve as milestones on your career path.

Research and explore. Try to understand the industry or field you're interested in. Learn about the job market, emerging trends, and potential opportunities. Seek informational interviews, job shadowing, internships, or consultancies to gain firsthand insights into different career paths. This exploration will help you make informed decisions throughout your career.

Keep adapting and refining. Remember that your career vision will evolve as you gain new experiences and insights. It's not that life might intrude; it *will* intrude and throw you massive curveballs. Be open to adjusting and refining your vision as needed. Stay flexible and adapt to changing circumstances or opportunities that may arise. One of the main reasons my former clients check back in with me is that their life circumstances have shifted their thinking, with new interests and needs becoming priorities.

When we're solely fixed on a specific outcome, we disconnect from the process and increase the chance of missing possibilities, solutions, and surprises. Your goal shouldn't be to rush through life, as you may miss it altogether. You should aim to find meaning and joy in everyday moments and to transmute failures into learning experiences. Many of the people we admire didn't get there by talent alone. They got there by learning to love the process of getting there. Focusing on a stepwise process makes us more likely to arrive at a desired outcome.

Implementing Your Strategy

The chapters in part III are the most transactional and include key implementation elements—your paperwork, online presence, professional network, and the interpersonal effectiveness needed to interview and negotiate with your potential future employer.

Your paperwork is not just your résumé, CV, or cover letter. Chapter 8 explored the ecosystem of documents in your career strategy. We investigated the happy file, professional paperwork, CVs, résumés, and cover letters. Consider reviewing and updating these documents at least once a year. Making an early investment in this system (and then regularly maintaining it) will make it easier for you to be one of the first applicants for the job, showing up with the most robust application.

Many professionals I talk with are resistant to being active on social media. As of this writing, the only one I strongly recommend is LinkedIn. Because so many recruiters use it, it is essential to have a landing page. Your profile reflects your résumé, so you should check on it perhaps monthly, moving a word or two around in the headlines to ensure it's picked up by LinkedIn's algorithm.

The networking conversation in chapter 10 is critical to having a flexible, successful career in global health. Global health business is done through alliances and collaborations, so it is time to get used to it. Be patient as you build your professional network. Start early in your career, and consistently keep track of your network, either in your phone contacts or by using some other software. Some people use client management systems to keep their networks updated and accessible. Don't wait until you need a favor to contact someone in your network. Communicate every so often, offering some tidbit of value, an update on your professional life, or a "congratulations" on one of their wins.

In the concluding chapter, we discussed what many consider first in their career planning: interpersonal communication with the potential employer. This includes informational interviews, pre-interviews, official interviews, and what happens during the negotiation process. All these interactions require preparation, research, and an awake inner observer who is calm, confident, and compassionate. For many, this is career development's most challenging and stressful part. Yet all of these activities can be mastered and made uniquely yours with knowledge and practice.

As a savvy career strategist, you will check in and fine-tune your planning for the rest of your professional life, repeating this process occasionally. Sometimes, the dream job is different from the next, but the next role is something you can prepare for. That is why strategic career planning is so critical to success. Because you now know how to do internal and external research, you understand what matters to you. With a clear vision and known preferences, you can scope out a potential position's location, job title and responsibilities, company history and values, benefits, salary, work hours, workplace culture and environment, work-life balance and workplace flexibility, professional development and advancement, employee appreciation and recognition, the team and management, tools and technology, and communication.

So, what happens next? The most common reactions to career planning are trepidation, excitement, and being overwhelmed. How you react to taking the next career step is unique to you, and I wanted to write a book that would serve the readers wherever they were in the process. I aimed to provide you with much food for thought and a step-by-step template for putting everything together. All this content is meant to support your creation of a lifelong career strategy. It is a personal and ongoing process. It requires self-reflection, exploration, and a willingness to embrace growth and change. Regularly reassess your vision and adjust as you gain new experiences and insights.

Reader, there is no one else like you. Your mosaic of knowledge, attitudes, skills, experience, and personal history is unlike anyone else's. Your story is your own, so your professional strategy must be created uniquely for you. I love my clients because they want to do work that matters. I wrote this book with love in my heart for all those who care about the suffering of others and desire to use their gifts—which we all have—to make a difference while living their best lives. You got this!

APPENDIX A

Turning an Unintentional Thought
into an Intentional One

After you have identified your circumstance, thought, feeling, action, and result in the below table, note the unintentional thought and create an intentional thought. Then, use the following questions to reflect on both thoughts. This activity will help you go deeper into the change process. Then practice, practice, practice the intentional thought until it settles in as something that is true.

Unintentional thought: _____

Intentional thought: _____

Look at the model you've developed and reflect on the following questions:

- How do I feel when I think this thought?
- How do I act when I think this thought?
- What is the result of my actions when I think this thought?
- What if I learned how to experience that feeling and learn to be with myself through the feeling while I made different choices in my thinking?

Table A.1. Circumstance, Thought, Feeling, Action, and Result

Circumstance

Thought

Feeling

Action

Result

Global Health and International Development
Job Websites

AidBoard
  http://www.aidboard.com

American Public Health Association
  www.apha.org

Association of Schools and Programs of Public Health
  https://publichealthjobs.aspph.org/

Career Builder
  www.careerbuilder.com

Child Family Health International
  www.cfhi.org

Communication Initiative Network
  www.comminit.com/job_vacancies

Consortium of Universities for Global Health
  (also a good resource for graduate programs)
  www.cugh.org

Core Group (networking)
www.coregroup.org

Devex Newswire
https://www.devex.com/jobs/search

DevNet Jobs
www.devnetjobs.org

Food and Agriculture Organization of the United Nations
www.fao.org/employment

Generation Next Humanitarian Fellowship Program
www.generationnextfellowship.org

Glassdoor
www.glassdoor.com

Global Health Council
https://globalhealth.org/job-board/

Global Health Jobs
www.globalhealthjobs.com

Global Health Science and Practice Journal
www.ghspjoural.org

Global Health Training, Advisory and Support Project
www.ghtasc.org

Global Jobs
www.globaljobs.org

Health Information and Publications Network (networking)
www.hipnet.org

Humentum
https://jobs.humentum.org

Idealist (also a good resource for graduate programs)
www.idealist.org

Indeed
  www.indeed.com

InterAction's *Monthly Development Magazine* (networking)
  www.interaction.org

International Career Employment Weekly
  www.internationaljobs.org

International Organization Careers of the UN Secretariat Associates Expert
  Program (including short-term assignments)
  www.iocareers.state.gov/

International Section, Student Assembly of the American Public Health
  Association
  www.apha.org

Jobs for Development
  https://ocs.fas.harvard.edu/links?jobs4development

LinkedIn
  Linkedin.com

MedAir
  www.medair.org

Monster
  www.monster.com

Public Health Employment Connection
  https:apps.sph.emory.edu/PHEC

Public Health Institute: includes sustaining technical and analytical
  resources (STAR) and global health technical professional (GHTP)
  vacancies, as well as internships
  www.PHI.org

ReliefWeb
  www.reliefweb.int/jobs

Sharon Rudy
www.drsharonrudy.com

USAID
www.usaid.gov/careers/hiring-mechanisms

User's Guide to USAID Health Programs
http://www.usaid.gov/what-we-do/global-health/global-health-users
-guide

Versatile PhD
www.versatilephd.com

YOUR NAME and Degree *(largest font here)*

City and State/Phone Number/Email Address/LinkedIn URL

(no street address, add any social media that reflects well on your professional life and "brand")

Expertise

List keywords that reflect your vision, the desired position, and are likely to be picked up by scanners and algorithms.

X	X	X	X
X	X	X	X
X	X	X	X

Career Highlights

Provide two to four key accomplishments that relate your desired position and reflect your expertise. Be sure to use metrics and data.

Work Experience

Start with your most recent position and include:

Position Title, Organization Name, Location, Month/Year—Present

- *Include four to six bulleted activities. Use action verbs. Use metrics as much as possible.*
- *X*
- *X*
- *X*
- *X*

Position Title, Organization Name, Location, Month/Year—Present

- *X*
- *X*
- *X*
- *X*
- *X*

Position Title, Organization Name, Location, Month/Year—Present

- *X*
- *X*
- *X*
- *X*
- *X*

Position Title, Organization Name, Location, Month/Year—Present

- *X*
- *X*
- *X*
- *X*
- *X*

Education

Most recent degree, degree content, educational institution, location (do not use date).

Your list should end with the first four-year degree.

Certifications/Licenses

Include this section based on relevancy to the desired position.

Illustrative List of Publications and Presentations

Start with your most recent publications and presentations. If numerous, use an illustrative list (draw from your source document—your CV). Generally, for your résumé, do not include:

- Street address
- An objective
- Jobs older than ten to fifteen years
- Anything that isn't relevant to your vision, experience, or the job description
- Jargon, acronyms, or initials
- Anything that isn't true
- Gaps less than a year or more than five years ago
- References
- Soft skills or adjectives that you can't back up with metrics. The purpose of the résumé is to get the interview, not necessarily the job.

FURTHER READING

Introduction

AARP Foundation. (2024). Back to Work 50+. Accessed May 6, 2024, https://www.aarp.org/aarp-foundation/our-work/income/back-to-work-50-plus/.

Fantom, N., Fu, H., Prince, & W. C. (2014). LICs, LMICs, UMICs, and HICs: Classifying Economies for Analytical Purposes. World Bank Blogs, June 13, 2014. https://blogs.worldbank.org/en/opendata/lics-lmics-umics-and-hics-classifying-economies-analytical-purposes.

Frenk, J., Bhutta, Z. A., Chen, L. C. H., Cohen, J., Crisp, N., et al. (2010). Health Professionals for a New Century: Transforming Education to Strengthen Health Systems in an Interdependent World. *Lancet* 376 (9756): 1923–58. https://doi.org/10.1016/S0140-6736(10)61854-5.

Friedman, T. L. (2016). *Thank You for Being Late: An Optimist's Guide to Thriving in the Age of Accelerations*. Farrar, Straus and Giroux.

Health and Education Resource Centre. (2024). Resources Library. Accessed May 3, 2024, https://healtheducationresources.unesco.org/resources-library.

Morrison, J. S., Muir, J. A., Farley, J., Osterman, A., Hawes, S. E., Martin, K., & Holmes, K. K. (2016). *Global Health Programs and Partnerships*. Center for

Strategic and International Studies. https://www.csis.org/analysis/global
-health-programs-and-partnerships.

Pendell, R., & VanderHelm, S. Generation Disconnected: Data on Gen Z in the Workplace. Gallup, November 11, 2022. https://www.gallup.com /workplace/404693/generation-disconnected-data-gen-workplace.aspx.

Rudy, S., Wanchek, N., Godsted, D., Blackburn, M. L., & Mann, E. M. (2017). The PHI/GHFP-II Employers' Study: The Hidden Barriers between Domestic and Global Health Careers and Crucial Competencies for Success. *Annals of Global Health* 82 (6): 1001–9. https://doi.org/10.1016/j.aogh.2016.10.012.

Sharone, O. (2024). *The Stigma Trap: College-Educated, Experienced, and Long-Term Unemployed.* Oxford University Press.

Chapter 1. Global Health Definitions and Locally Led Development

Adams, V. (2021). Localization and Its Discontents: A Genealogy of Decoloniality in Global Health. *Global Public Health Publication* 16 (6): 840–52. doi:10.1080/17441692.2021.1898039.

Alayande, B. T. (2023). To Be Seen, Heard and Valued. Active Engagement as the Next Frontier for Global Health Conference Equity: A View from the Global South. *Journal of Public Health in Africa* doi:10.4081/jphia.2023 .2810.

Alesina, A., & Dollar, D. (2000). Who Gives Foreign Aid to Whom and Why? *Journal of Economic Growth* 5 (1): 33–63.

Aly, H. (2022). Ten Efforts to Decolonize Aid. New Humanitarian, August 12, 2022. https://www.thenewhumanitarian.org/feature/2-022/08/12/10-efforts -to-decolonize-aid.

Anderson, W. (2006). *Colonial Pathologies: American Tropical Medicine, Race, and Hygiene in the Philippines.* Duke University Press.

Arnold, D., Pati, B., & Harrison, M. (2016). *Medicine and Colonialism: Historical Perspectives in India and South Africa.* Routledge.

Burke, R. (2010). *Decolonization and the Evolution of International Human Rights.* University of Pennsylvania Press

Chipembere, E. (2023). *NNGO Voices: Leader Perspectives on Locally-Led Development.* Humentum.

Choonara, S., Wilkinson, A., Bates, I., & McCoy, D. (2020). Decolonizing Global Health: If Not Now, When? *BMJ Global Health* 5 (8): https://gh.bmj.com/content/5/8/e003394.

Cohen, M. N. (1989). *Health and the Rise of Civilization*. Yale University Press.

Crane, J. T. (2010). Unequal Partners: AIDS, Academia, and the Rise of Global Health. *Behometh: A Journal on Civilization* 3. https://cpb-us-e1.wpmucdn.com/blogs.uoregon.edu/dist/5/8794/files/2014/08/Unequal-Partners-y6xti4.pdf.

Davis, D. K. (1983). *Medicine and Power in Tunisia, 1780–1900*. Cambridge University Press.

Decker, C., & McMahon, E. (2020). *The Idea of Development in Africa: A History*. Cambridge University Press.

Devex. (2022). *The Localization Agenda: A Devex Pro Special Report*. Devex.

El Bcheraoui, C., & Mokdad, A. H. (2020). Decolonizing Global Health: If Not Now, When? *American Journal of Public Health* 110 (9): 1293–94. doi:10.2105/AJPH.2020.305851.

Finkel, M. L., Temmermann, M. Suleman, F., Barry, M. Salm, M., Binagwaho, A., Kilmarx, & P. H. (2022). What Do Global Health Practitioners Think about Decolonizing Global Health? *Annals of Global Health* 88 (1): 61. doi:10.5334/aogh.3714.

Frank, S. (2022). Why Decolonizing Philanthropy Is Important Now More Than Ever and How to Achieve It. Business Fights Poverty (*blog*), May 11, 2022. https://businessfightspoverty.org/why-decolonizing-philanthropy-is-important-now-more-than-ever-and-how-to-achieve-it/.

Friedman, T. L. (2016). *Thank You for Being Late: An Optimist's Guide to Thriving in the Age of Accelerations*. Farrar, Straus and Giroux.

Garcia-Elorrio, E., Rowe, S., Teijeiro, M., Ciapponi, A., & Rowe, A. (2019). The Effectiveness of the Quality Improvement Collaborative Strategy in Low- and Middle-Income Countries: A Systematic Review and Meta-Analysis. *PLoS One* 14 (10): e0221919.

Gibson, C., & Bokoff, J. (2018). *Deciding Together: Shifting the Power and Resources through Participatory Grantmaking*. Grantcraft Foundation Centre.

Grace, B., & Allen, R. R. (2020). The "How" of Shifting Power: Transformation in the Context of Responsible Transition Processes. Stopping as

Success (*blog*), November 23, 2020. https://www.stoppingassuccess.org
/the-how-of-shifting-power-transformations-in-the-context-of
-responsible-transition-processes/.

Hansoti, B., Schleiff, M., Akridge, A., Dolive, C., Gordon, A., et al. (2020).
Developing a High-Impact Learning Program for Global Health Professionals: The STAR Project. *Pedagogy in Health Promotion* 6 (1): 23–30.

Horton, R. (2021). Offline: Decolonization and the Demand for a Just
Memory. *Lancet* 398 (10313): 1787.

———. (2021). Offline: The Myth of "Decolonizing Global Health." *Lancet*
398 (10312): 1673.

Kaplan, R. M., Spittel, M. L., David, D. H., & Peterson, C. (2009). Health and
Globalization. *Lancet* 373 (9679): 434–35. doi:10.1016/
s0140-6736(09)60144-7.

Kirmayer, L. J., Gone, J. P., & Moses, J. (2014). Decolonizing Global Health:
Transdisciplinary Approaches to Understanding Indigenous Health
Inequities. *Transcultural Psychiatry* 51 (6): 850–72.
doi:10.1177/1363461514539752.

Kumar, R. (2019). *The Business of Changing the World: How Billionaires, Tech
Disrupters, and Social Entrepreneurs Are Transforming the Global Aid
Industry*. Beacon Press.

Lachenal, G. (2002). Colonialism and Public Health: The Case of the Yaws
Eradication Program in the French Colonial Empire. *Comparative Studies
in Society and History* 44 (4): 834–59. doi:10.1017/S0010417502000383.

Lambe, R. J. (2019). Race, Colonialism, and the Evolution of French Al-
zheimer's Disease Research. *Journal of the History of Medicine and Allied
Sciences* 74 (1): 32–52. doi:10.1093/jhmas/jry057.

Lankenau, B., Stefan, M. D. (2013). Public Health, NCDs, Health Promotion,
and Business Partnering: Benefits, Concerns, Remedies, and Moving
towards Creative Partnering. In *Global Handbook on Noncommunicable
Diseases and Health Promotion*, edited by D. V. McQueen, 345–63.
Springer. https://doi.org/10.1007/978-1-4614-7594-1_23.

Mintz, S. W. (1986). *Sacred Gifts, Profane Pleasures: A History of Tobacco and
Chocolate in the Atlantic World*. Cornell University Press.

Newland, J. (2022). Nurses Are Everywhere around the Globe. *Nurse Practitioner* 47 (5): 9. https://doi.org/10.1097/01.npr.0000827048.70857.ec.

Niyonkuru, F. (2016). Failure of Foreign Aid in Developing Countries: A Quest for Alternatives. *Business and Economics Journal* 7 (3): 1–9.

Nyasulu, G. (2009). The Design and Implementation of Effective Poverty Eradication Programs: The Rights-Based Approach. PhD dissertation, James Cook University. http://eprints.jcu.edu.au/10535/.

Pan American Health Organization. (2023). Strengthening Primary Care, Harnessing New Health Technologies Key to Better Pandemic Recovery and Preparedness, PAHO Director Says. PAHO, April 13, 2023. https://www.paho.org/en/news/13-4-2023-strengthening-primary-care-harnessing-new-health-technologies-key-better-pandemic.

Rudy, S., Wanchek, N., Godsted, D., Blackburn, M. L., & Mann, E. M. (2017). The PHI/GHFP-II Employers' Study: The Hidden Barriers between Domestic and Global Health Careers and Crucial Competencies for Success. *Annals of Global Health* 82 (6): 1001–9. https://doi.org/10.1016/j.aogh.2016.10.012.

Serafin, R., & Tennyson, R. (2018). Power Shifts when Power Is Shared: Re-Framing the Role of Donors in Development. Global Alliance for Community Philanthropy. https://www.academia.edu/78302163/power_shifts-when-power-is-shared-re-framing-the-role-of-donors-in-development.

Spicer, N., Bhattacharya, D., Dimka, R., & Sen, N. (2019). Localization of Global Health: Unpacking Agency and Power Dynamics in Global Health Partnerships. *BMJ Global Health* 4 (5): doi:10.1136/bmjgh-2019-001282.

Tsai, A., & Tomori, O. (2020). Localizing Global Health: The Role of Multi-Level Multi-Stakeholder Partnerships in Response to the Ebola Epidemic in Western Africa. *Globalization and Health* 16 (1): 1–6. doi:10.1186/s12992-020-00559-9.

Tuck, E., & Yang, K. W. (2012). Decolonization Is Not a Metaphor. *Decolonization: Indigeneity, Education and Society* 1 (1): 1–40.

US Agency for International Development. (2021). *Local Capacity Development Policy*, Version 8. USAID.

———. (2023). *Partners in Localization: Designing for Change: Workshop Summary Report.* USAID.

Vallesi, S., Wood, L., Dimer, L., & Zada, M. (2018). "In Their Own Voice": Incorporating Underlying Social Determinants into Aboriginal Health Promotion Programs. *International Journal of Environmental Research and Public Health* 15 (7): 1514.

Vaughan, M. (1996). *Colonial Medicine and Indigenous Health: Central Africa in the Belgian Congo Era.* Cambridge University Press.

West Africa Society Institute. (2023). *Decolonising Aid: Perspectives from Civil Society in Francophone sub-Saharan Africa.* WASCI.

Chapter 2. Key Competencies in Global Health

Cherniak, W., Nezami, E., Eichbaum, Q., Evert, J., Doobay-Persaud, A., Rudy, S., DeFrank, G., Hall, T., & Hoverman, A. (2019). Employment Opportunities and Experiences among Recent Master's-Level Global Health Graduates. *Annals of Global Health* 85 (1): 31. doi:10.5334/aogh.305.

Consortium of Universities for Global Health. (2024). Global Health Competencies Toolkit. Accessed May 3, 2024, https://www.cugh.org/online-tools /competencies-toolkit/.

DiPrete-Brown, L. (2014). Towards Defining Interprofessional Competencies for Global Health Education: Drawing on Educational Frameworks and the Experience of the UW-Madison Global Health Institute. *Journal of Law, Medicine, and Ethics* 42 (2): 32.

Friedman, T. L. (2016). *Thank You for Being Late: An Optimist's Guide to Thriving in the Age of Accelerations.* Farrar, Straus and Giroux.

Fuller, R. B. (1975). *Synergetics: Explorations in the Geometry of Thinking.* Macmillan.

Hansoti, B., Schleiff, M., Akridge, A., Dolive, C., Gordon, A., et al. (2020). Developing a High-Impact Learning Program for Global Health Professionals: The STAR Project. *Pedagogy in Health Promotion* 6 (1): 23–30.

Institute of Medicine. (2009). *The US Commitment to Global Health: Recommendations for the Public and Private Sectors.* Institute of Medicine Committee on the US Commitment to Global Health.

Jogerst, K., Callender, B., Adams, V., Evert, J., Fields, E., et al. Identifying Interprofessional Global Health Competencies for 21st-Century Health Professionals. *Annals of Global Health* 81 (2): 239–47.

Kabat-Zinn, J. (1990). *Full Catastrophe Living: Using the Wisdom of Your Body and Mind to Face Stress, Pain, and Illness*. Delta.

Longhurst, R., & Choi, W. (2023). What the Next Generation of Project Management Will Look Like. *Harvard Business Review*, November 6, 2023.

McCown, D., Reibel, D., & Micozzi, M. S. (2010). *Teaching Mindfulness: A Practical Guide for Clinicians and Educators*. Springer.

Rudy, S., & Gordon, A. (2018). Global Health Professional Skills and Careers. In L. D. Brown (Ed.), *Foundations for Global Health Practice*. Jossey-Bass.

Rudy, S., & Petroni, S. (2014). Careers in Public Health Educational and Environmental NGOs. In L. E. Cressey, B. Helmer, & J. E. Steffensen (Eds.), *Careers in International Affairs*, 9th ed.. School of Foreign Service, Georgetown University.

Rudy, S., Wanchek, N., Godsted, D., Blackburn, M. L., & Mann, E. M. (2017). The PHI/GHFP-II Employers' Study: The Hidden Barriers between Domestic and Global Health Careers and Crucial Competencies for Success. *Annals of Global Health* 82 (6): 1001–9. https://doi.org/10.1016/j.aogh.2016.10.012.

Schieiff, M., Hansoti, B., Akridge, A., Dolive, C., Hausner, D., Kalbarczyk, A., Pariyo, G., Quinn, T., Rudy, S., & Bennett, S. (2020). Implementation of Global Health Competencies: A Scoping Review on Target Audiences, Level, and Pedagogy and Assessment Strategies. *PLOS One*, October 1, 2020. https:/doi.org/10.1371/journal.pone.0239917.

World Health Organization. (2002). *The World Health Report: Reducing Risks, Promoting Healthy Life*, https://www.who.int/publications/i/item/9241562072.

———. (2020). *IBP Network: Current Project Brief*. WHO. www.who.int/publications/m/item/ibp-network for Implementing Best Practices Network.

———. (2024). WHO Mortality Database: Interactive Platform Visualizing Mortality Data. Accessed May 3, 2024, https://platform.who.int/mortality.

Chapter 3. Career Considerations across the Lifespan

Cherniak, W., Nezami, E., Eichbaum, Q., Evert, J., Doobay-Persaud, A., Rudy, S., DeFrank, G., Hall, T., & Hoverman, A. (2019). Employment Opportunities and Experiences among Recent Master's-Level Global Health Graduates. *Annals of Global Health* 85 (1): 31. doi:10.5334/aogh.305.

Drain, P., Mock, C., Toole, D., Rosenwald, A., Hehn, M. Csordas, T., Ferguson, L., Waggett, C., Obidoa, C., & Wasserheit, J. N. (2017). The Emergence of Undergraduate Majors in Global Health: Systematic Review of Programs and Recommendations for Future Directions. *American Journal of Tropical Medicine and Hygiene* 96 (1): 16–23.

Rudy, S., Wanchek, N., Godsted, D., Blackburn, M. L., & Mann, E. M. (2017). The PHI/GHFP-II Employers' Study: The Hidden Barriers between Domestic and Global Health Careers and Crucial Competencies for Success. *Annals of Global Health* 82 (6): 1001–9. https://doi.org/10.1016/j.aogh.2016.10.012.

Rudy, S., Wanchek, N., George, J., & Kaindi, J. (2019). *The Cross-Over Study: Facilitators, Obstacles and Strategies to Move between Domestic and Global Health Careers.* USAID/Public Health Institute, 2019

Chapter 4. Building the Foundation by Knowing Where You Are Now

Céré, J. (2006). Advertising and the End of the World. Thinkful (*blog*), October 17, 2006. http://www.thinkful.tv/2006/10/advertising-and-end-of-world.html.

Creswell, J. D., Pacilio, L. E., Lindsay, E. K., & Brown, K. W. (2014). Brief Mindfulness Meditation Training Alters Psychological and Neuroendocrine Responses to Social Evaluative Stress. *Psychoneuroendocrinology* 44: 1–12.

Goyal, M., Singh, S., Sibinga, E. M., Gould, N. F., Rowland-Seymour, et al. (2014). Meditation Programs for Psychological Stress and Well-Being: A Systematic Review and Meta-Analysis. *JAMA Internal Medicine* 174 (3): 357–68.

Grossman, P., Niemann, L., Schmidt, S., & Walach, H. (2004). Mindfulness-Based Stress Reduction and Health Benefits: A Meta-Analysis. *Journal of Psychosomatic Research* 57 (1): 35–43.

Hofmann, S. G., Sawyer, A. T., Witt, A. A., & Oh, D. (2010). The Effect of Mindfulness-Based Therapy on Anxiety and Depression: A Meta-Analytic Review. *Journal of Consulting and Clinical Psychology* 78 (2): 169–83.

Hölzel, B. K., Carmody, J., Vangel, M., Congleton, C., Yerramsetti, S. M., Gard, T., & Lazar, S. W. (2011). Mindfulness Practice Leads to Increases in Regional Brain Gray Matter Density. *Psychiatry Research: Neuroimaging* 191 (1): 36–43.

Kabat-Zinn, J. (1994). *Wherever You Go, There You Are: Mindfulness Meditation in Everyday Life.* Hachette Books.

Karpicke, J. D., & Roediger, H. L., III. (2008). The Critical Importance of Retrieval for Learning. *Science* 319 (5865): 966–68.

Keng, S. L., Smoski, M. J., & Robins, C. J. (2011). Effects of Mindfulness on Psychological Health: A Review of Empirical Studies. *Clinical Psychology Review* 31 (6): 1041–56.

Mueller, P. A., & Oppenheimer, D. M. (2014). The Pen Is Mightier Than the Keyboard: Advantages of Longhand over Laptop Note-Taking. *Psychological Science* 25 (6): 1159–68.

Rozin, P., & Royzman, E. B. (2001). Negativity Bias, Negativity Dominance, and Contagion. *Personality and Social Psychology Review* 5 (4): 296–320.

Rozsa, M. (2021). WHO Official: It Is "Unrealistic" to Expect the Pandemic to be Over by the End of 2021. Salon, March 3, 2021. https://www.salon.com /2021/03/03/who-official-it-is-unrealistic-to-expect-pandemic-to-be-over -by-end-of-2021/.

Rudy, S., Wanchek, N., Godsted, D., Blackburn, M. L., & Mann, E. M. (2017). The PHI/GHFP-II Employers' Study: The Hidden Barriers between Domestic and Global Health Careers and Crucial Competencies for Success. *Annals of Global Health* 82 (6): 1001–9. https://doi.org/10.1016/j.aogh.2016 .10.012.

Vaish, A., Grossmann, T., & Woodward, A. (2008). Not All Emotions Are Created Equal: The Negativity Bias in Social-Emotional Development. *Psychological Bulletin* 134 (3): 383–403.

Wigert, B. (2022). The Future of Hybrid Work: 5 Key Questions Answered with Data. Gallup, March 15, 2022. Gallup.com.workplace>360632>future >hybrid>work>key>questions>answered>data.ASPX.

Chapter 5. Creating the Vision

Covey, S. R. (1989). *The 7 Habits of Highly Effective People*. Free Press / Simon & Schuster.

Dweck, C. S. (2016). *Mindset: The New Psychology of Success*. Random House.

Locke, E. A., & Latham, G. P. (1990). *A Theory of Goal Setting and Task Performance*. Prentice Hall.

Manalo, M. (2024). Mindset of an Entrepreneur: 5 Important Lessons to Learn. HICAPS, accessed May 4, 2024. https://hicaps.com.ph/mindset-of-an-entrepreneur/.

Robbins, T. (1991). *Awaken the Giant Within*. Free Press / Simon & Schuster.

Sharma, R. S. (1999). *The Monk Who Sold His Ferrari: A Fable about Fulfilling Your Dreams and Reaching Your Destiny*. Harper.

Tolle, E. (1997). *The Power of Now*. New World Library.

Chapter 6. Identifying the Gaps

Any.do. (2022). Productivity Shame and How to Fight It. Any.do (*blog*), December 27, 2022. https://www.any.do/blog/productivity-shame-and-how-to-fight-it/.

Au-Yeung, J. (2022). Three Ways to Break Bad Habits. Front End Dev, May 16, 2022. https://frontenddev.info/three-ways-to-break-bad-habits/.

Bandura, A. (1961). Behavioral Modification through Modeling Procedures. In L. Krasner & L. P. Ullmann (Eds.), *Research in Behavior Modification* (pp. 305–40). Holt, Rinehart, and Winston.

Beck, A. T. (1976). *Cognitive Therapy and the Emotional Disorders*. Penguin.

Chang, M. (2023). Goal Setting and Productivity Tips for Professionals. Pierre Henry Socks, June 11, 2023. https://pierrehenrysocks.com/blogs/socks/goal-setting-and-productivity-tips-for-professionals.

Clear, J. (2018). *Atomic Habits: An Easy and Proven Way to Build Good Habits and Break Bad Ones*. Avery.

Cognitive Science Career Paths. (2023). Virtual Clinic vs Virtual Hospital (Virtual Reality Cognitive Therapy Tips). July 2, 2023, https://carlsonlab.org/virtual-clinic-vs-virtual-hospital-virtual-reality-cognitive-therapy-tips/.

Duckworth, A. (2016). *Grit: The Power of Passion and Perseverance*. Scribner.

Duhigg, C. (2016). *Smarter Faster Better: The Secrets of Being Productive in Life and Business*. Random House.

Dweck, C. S. (2007). *Mindset: The New Psychology of Success*. Ballantine.

Ellis, A. (1962). *Reason and Emotion in Psychotherapy*. Lyle Stuart.

Fleishman, E. A. (1969). Some Issues in the Measurement of Goal-Traits Relationships in Applied Research. *Organizational Behavior and Human Performance* 4 (4): 355–67.

Hyatt, M. (2018). *Your Best Year Ever: A 5-Step Plan for Achieving Your Most Important Goals*. Baker Books.

Keller, G., & Papasan, J. (2013). *The One Thing: The Surprisingly Simple Truth behind Extraordinary Results*. Bard Press.

Locke, E. A. (1968). Toward a Theory of Task Motivation and Incentives. *Organizational Behavior and Human Performance* 3 (2): 157–89.

Neff, K. D., & Germer, C. K. (2018). *The Mindful Self-Compassion Workbook: A Proven Way to Accept Yourself, Build Inner Strength, and Thrive*. Guilford Press.

Schwartz, D. J. (1987). *The Magic of Thinking Big*. Simon & Schuster.

Segal, Z. V., Williams, J. M. G., & Teasdale, J. D. (2002). *Mindfulness-Based Cognitive Therapy for Depression: A New Approach to Preventing Relapse*. Guilford Press.

Shahhian, S. (2023). What Is Trauma Focused Cognitive Behavioral Therapy? Liberty Psychological Association (*blog*), May 22, 2023. https://shervanshahhian.com/2023/05/22/what-is-trauma-focused-cognitive-behavioral-therapy/.

Simi Valley Adult School and Career Institute. (2024). Navigating Career Transitions: Leverage Skills and Succeed. Accessed May 5, 2024, https://simivalleyadultschool.org/blog/career-transitions-leverage-skills-success.

Tracy, B. (2003). *Goals! How to Get Everything You Want—Faster Than You Ever Thought Possible*. Berrett-Koehler.

———. (2007). *Eat That Frog! 21 Great Ways to Stop Procrastinating and Get More Done in Less Time*. Berrett-Koehler.

Yukl, G., & Latham, G. P. (1978). Interactions between Goal Setting and Leadership in Field Settings. *Journal of Applied Psychology* 63 (4): 428–32.

Chapter 7. Goal Setting

Clear, James. (2018). *Atomic Habits: An Easy and Proven Way to Build Good Habits and Break Bad Ones*. Avery.

Latham, G. P., & Locke, E. A. (2006). Enhancing the Benefits and Overcoming the Pitfalls of Goal Setting. *Organizational Dynamics* 35 (4): 332–40.

Matthews, Gail. (2007). The Impact of Commitment, Accountability, and Written Goals on Goal Achievement. *Psychology/Faculty Presentations* 3: https://scholar.dominican.edu/psychology-faculty-conference-presentation/3.

Chapter 8. Creating Your Professional Records System

Betz, Ann. Neuroscience of Coaching. Coaching.com, accessed June 4, 2024. https://www.coaching.com/neuroscience/program/

Canada's Credit Unions. (2024). Tips and Strategies for Graduating Students. Accessed May 5, 2024, https://canadascreditunions.ca/tips-and-strategies-for-graduating-students/.

Cole, Michael S., Robert S. Rubin, Hubert S. Feild, & William F. Giles. (2007). Recruiters' Perceptions and Use of Applicant Résumé Information: Screening the Recent Graduate. *Applied Psychology* 56 (2).

CV Blade. (2024). Reimbursement Manager Resume Example and Writing Guide. Accessed May 5, 2024, https://cvblade.com/resume-examples/reimbursement-manager/.

Ladders. (2018). *Eye-Tracking Study*. Ladders. https://www.theladders.com/static/images/basicSite/pdfs/TheLadders-EyeTracking-StudyC2.pdf.

Lowery, T., & Thomason, R. (2016). Résumé Faux Pas and Job Searching Fatigue: An Examination of the Hiring Process. *Journal of Applied Business and Economics* 18 (4): 25–36.

O'Donnell, R. (2018). Eye Tracking Study Shows Recruiters Look at Resumes for 7 Seconds. HR Dive, November 18, 2018. https://www.hrdive.com/news/eye-tracking-study-shows-recruiters-look-at-resumes-for-7-seconds/541582/.

Siegel, D. (2016). *Mind: A Journey to the Heart of Being Human*. Norton Series on Interpersonal Biology. W. W. Norton.

Solberg, C. C., & Fazio, J. C. (2016). The Effects of Resume Characteristics on Interviewer Hiring Recommendations: An Exploratory Study. *Journal of Applied Business and Economics* 18 (4): 25–36.

Stay on Search. (2024). Understanding Social Networking Demographics. Accessed June 4, 2024, https://www.stayonsearch.com/understanding -social-networking-demographics.

Thompson, J. M., et al. (2016). A Content Analysis of Entry-Level Job Qualifications: What Skills and Attributes Are Employers Seeking? *Journal of Employment Counseling* 53 (4): 146–58.

Zielinski, Dave. (2011). Automated Tracking Systems Evolve. Society for Human Resource Management, May 27, 2011. https://www.shrm.org /topics-tools/news/technology/applicant-tracking-systems-evolve.

———. (2024). Automated Tools Can Help Keep Pace with Regulatory Changes. Society for Human Resource Management, April 22, 2024. https://www.shrm.org/topics-tools/news/technology/automated-tools -keep-pace-regulatory-changes.

Chapter 9. Your Online Presence

Altabba, K. (2021). Editing Your Profile Picture. Pivotino, August 2, 2021. https://tutorial.pivotino.com/tutorial/pivoguides-1/editing-your-profile -picture-8.

Business Allies. Growing Your Network: Targeted Approaches to Expand Business Connections. Accessed May 5, 2024, https://vaallies.org /growing-your-network-targeted-approaches-to-expand-business -connections/.

HireQuotient. What Is External Recruitment? June 6, 2023, https://www .hirequotient.com/blog/what-is-external-recruitment.

Kandas, M. (2023). Mastering Networking: Tips to Expand and Maintain Your Professional Network. Revenue and Profit, June 20, 2023. https:// revenuesandprofits.com/mastering-networking-tips-to-expand-and -maintain-your-professional-network/.

Liu, J. (2024). The Career Relaunch (*blog*). Accessed May 5, 2024, https:// josephliu.co/category/social-media/.

Chapter 10. Creating a Professional Networking System That Keeps on Giving

Daniels, D. (2009). *The Essential Enneagram: The Definitive Personality Test and Self-Discovery Guide*. HarperOne.

Evans, J. (2023). How To Start Networking. NetworkingJean, June 8, 2023. https://networkingjean.ie/how-to-start-networking/.

Gelbard, S. (2023). How to Manage Your Expectations of Your Mentor. September 13, 2023, https://scottgelbard.us/how-to-manage-your -expectations-of-your-mentor/.

Harris, Jason. (2021). Never Let Your Work Relationships Drop. Fast Company, October 28, 2021. https://www.fastcompany.com/90690750/never -let-your-work-relationships-drop-here-are-4-ways-to-make-sure-you -dont-lose-them.

Leading Ladies Africa. (2023). The Power of Networking: 7 Tips on Building Strong Professional Connections. August 28, 2023, https:// leadingladiesafrica.org/the-power-of-networking-7-tips-on-building -strong-professional-connections/.

MacIntyre, P. L. (2020). Supporting Career Choices for Women in the Sciences and Engineering. *Academic Journal of Engineering Studies*. https://crimsonpublishers.com/aes/fulltext/AES.000510.php.

Moran, A. (2022). Maintain Bonds with Coworkers Even While Remote. *Washington Post*, February 28, 2022. https://jobs.washingtonpost.com /article/maintain-bonds-with-coworkers-even-while-remote/?keywords =Zoom.

Palmer, H. (1995). *The Enneagram in Love and Work: Understanding Your Intimate and Business Relationships*. HarperCollins.

Piyush. (2023). Where to Find Expert Guidance for Digital Marketing with Google AdWords in Delhi? Perfect eLearning, June 23, 2023. https:// perfectelearning.com/blog/where-to-find-expert-guidance-for-digital -marketing.

Shah, R. (2023). How to Network Effectively to Advance Your Career. Indeed Finance, April 20, 2023. https://indeedfinance.com/en/how-to-network -effectively-to-advance-your-career/.

Skillabilly. (2023). The Role of Mentoring and Coaching in Career Development. August 31, 2023, https://www.skillabilly.com/the-role-of
-mentoring-and-coaching-in-career-development/.

Chapter 11. Interacting with Potential Employers and Coworkers

Allen, David. (2015). *Getting Things Done: The Art of Stress-Free Productivity*. Penguin.

Dunlap, Tori. (2022). *Financial Feminist: Overcome the Patriarchy's Bullsh*t to Master Your Money and Build a Life You Love*. Dey Street Books.

O'Donnell, J. T. (2024). Never Accept a Job Offer until You Do This. Work It Daily, February 2, 2024. https://www.workitdaily.com/do-before
-accepting-job-offer.

Sandberg, S. (2013). *Lean In: Women, Work and the Will to Lead*. GoldenHouse. https://book.goldenhouse.com.my/shop/english-books/lifestyle/lean-in
-women-work-and-the-will-to-lead/.

Smart Locus. (2023). Purpose: The Guiding Light to a Fulfilling and Meaningful Life. August 22, 2023, https://smartlocus.in/purpose-the-guiding
-light-to-a-fulfilling-and-meaningful-life/.

Stange, J. (2023). Connecting Your Platform to Your Greater Mission. Platform Launchers, June 13, 2023. https://www.platformlaunchers.com
/blog/connecting-your-platform-to-your-greater-mission.

Tu, Vivian. (2023). *Rich AF: The Winning Money Mindset That Will Change Your Life*. Portfolio.

business case, 48
business-of-one strategy, 3, 4, 14–15, 74, 78, 127, 181, 192, 193; for graduate school selection, 71–72; market information in, 94; social media use in, 19, 146
buybacks, 180–81

Canva, 133
capacity building and sustainability, 11, 27–28, 42, 68; in clinical research, 27, 46; donors' influence on, 36–37; LMIC professionals' role, 31, 35; USAID's role, 28, 32–33, 36, 46
CareerBuilder, 153
career paths, in global health, 18, 62–69, 78; personal preference aspect, 70–71. *See also* career transitions; direct service careers; monitoring and evaluation (M&E); program implementation; research
career transitions, 6–8, 13–17; midcareer and senior professionals, 73–76, 166. *See also* domestic-to-global career transitions
Castillo, Brooke, 106
Center for Strategic and International Studies, 10, 160
Centers for Disease Control and Prevention (CDC), 40, 92
Child Family Health International, 65
Clear, James, *Atomic Habits,* 120
climate change, 24–25, 44, 91
coaches/coaching, 4, 7, 8, 16, 61, 116, 118, 129, 157, 166, 177–78; academic training in, 71; self-coaching, 103–4, 106; TeamRudy LLC, 17. *See also* mentors/mentorship
Coalition for Epidemic Preparedness Innovations, 9
cognitive behavioral therapy (CBT) techniques, 83, 103–14
cognitive distortions. *See* thought distortions
collaboration, 195; competency, 41, 50, 71, 173–74, 175; deficits, 38–39, 71; global, 9, 56; interdisciplinary, 24; in knowledge sharing, 56, 57, 58
colleagues and coworkers: interactions with, 175–76; networking with, 159–60; potential, questions for, 179

colonialism, 28–30, 35, 103
communication: with clients, 71; cross-cultural, 13, 46, 133; interpersonal, 56; during job interviews, 178–79; as key competency, 38–39, 41, 45–46, 51, 56; with mentors, 164; mindfulness in, 52; in networking, 156–58; post-interview, 19; in project management, 48; skill deficits, 38–39, 71; small talk, 157–58, 172; social and behavioral, 14; in work environment, 170–71. *See also* interpersonal effectiveness
Comparably website, 180, 184–85
compensation package. *See* benefits and compensation
competency clusters, in global health, 17–18, 38–59, 70, 192–93; academic training in, 71; employers' evaluation, 38–40, 43; knowledge management, 42, 53, 56–59, 101; performance *versus,* 40; process and resource optimization, 41, 42, 101; professional capacity, 41, 42, 101; self-assessment of, 89–90. *See also* business, of global health; health expertise; intra- and interpersonal effectiveness; knowledge, attitudes, skills, and experiences
conferences, 14, 58, 81, 85, 99, 122, 157–58, 160
conflict-resolution strategies, 50, 173–74, 175
Consortium of Universities for Global Health, 10, 24, 39–40, 160; Competency Subcommittee, 41; Employers' Study, 39–40, 43; Global Health Fellows Program II, 41–42; STAR competency documentation, 39–40
consultants/consultancies, 3, 14, 17, 27, 51, 67, 89, 103, 131
continuous learning, 42, 57
contracting/contractors, 28, 50, 51, 132
corporations: influence on global health, 25–26; as work setting, 74
Council for African Family Studies, 61
counseling, 13–14, 16, 34, 60; academic training in, 13, 62–63, 71, 128–29

experience/expertise: diversity, 62; documentation of, 127–28; employers' requirements, 62, 102; gaps, 90, 102; learned, 130; overseas experience, 23, 60, 64–65, 74, 75, 90, 87, 102, 103, 192; overstatement, 170; as résumé component, 136; self-assessment, 88–89, 101. *See also* health expertise
extrovert personality, 158, 159
Eye-Tracking Study, 135, 138

Facebook, 137, 146, 187–88
family planning, 34, 86
Family Planning Association of Kenya, 89, 131
Fast Company, 159–60
feedback, 118, 149; during and after job interview, 171, 179; on goal achievement, 118; from mentors, 162, 163; in performance assessments, 174; positive and supportive, 89, 114
fellowship programs, 15–16, 38–39, 41–42, 70, 136–37, 168; failed applications, 75–76
Financial Feminist, 182
financial systems, technology-based, 47, 51
food insecurity, 44
foundation building, for global health careers, 77, 81–94, 116, 193–95; four key questions, 18, 84, 87–94, 102, 104–5, 193. *See also* inner observer; mindfulness; self-reflection
foundations (organizations), 16, 25, 26, 33, 35, 61, 69
Friedman, Thomas, *Thank You for Being Late,* 11, 31
Fuller, Buckminster, 56
funding, of global health initiatives: governmental approval, 32; lack of sustainable outcomes, 32; for locally-led development, 33–34, 35, 36–37; organizational support, 180; technology use in, 56

Gainesville Suicide and Crisis Prevention Center, 105–6
Gallup, 12, 146, 160
gap analysis, 99, 100–115, 116, 119–21
Gates Foundation, 25, 26, 35, 69

Gavi, 9
genocide, in Rwanda, 105–6
geographic location preferences, for global health careers, 89–91, 90, 170–71, 196
GH Council (GHC), 40
Glassdoor, 153, 180, 184
Global Burden of Disease Study (GBD), 92
Global Fund to Fight AIDS, Tuberculosis, and Malaria, 9
global health: definitions, 2, 23–25, 192; obstacles, 30; unmet needs, 93; workforce changes, 4
global health careers: factors affecting, 8–11; increased interest in, 12; negative aspects, 12; personal story of, 13–17; US *versus* overseas location, 9
global health career strategies, 1–3, 17–18, 23–78, 92; after job loss, 4, 13–14; annual checkup on, 123; client histories, 5–8; implementation of, 195–97; influence of significant others on, 6, 73–74, 77, 81, 99, 114, 118, 181; for non-global health professionals, 6–7, 13–14; as stepwise process, 191–94; unexpected situations in, 82–83. *See also* big-picture considerations; foundation building; lifespan career considerations; networking, professional
Global Health Council, 160, 202
Global Health Jobs, 153
global health programs, 8
globalization, 8–9, 11–12, 23–24, 31, 53–54, 70
Global Jobs, 153
Global Polio Eradication Initiative (GPEI), 10
Global South, 65
goal-setting, 4, 19, 53, 60–61, 68, 116–23; action plans, 121; emotional engagement in, 4, 19, 60–61, 68, 119; gap analysis, 99, 100–115, 116, 119–21; in locally-led development, 35–36; in mentor-mentee relationship, 162; obstacles, 18, 100, 120; for professional networking, 156; realistic and specific, 115, 117–18, 119–20; relation to vision/visioning, 96–98, 116–19, 193–94, 196; SMART goals, 119, 194; theory, 117; timelines, 117, 120, 122; writing and posting practice, 120–21
Google Docs, 134

graduate education, 69, 70–73, 192. *See also* master of public health (MPH)/master of health science (MHS)

grants and grant proposals, 15, 26, 46, 52, 72

gratitude journaling, 113

Gurdjieff, George, 159

happy file, 89, 109, 128–32, 144, 145, 195

hard skills, 135, 139, 149, 150. *See also* technical skills

headhunters, 19, 147

health, social and political determinants of, 63

health care: inequities, 23–25, 43, 47; medical model, 28–29, 63; sustainable programs, 47

health care systems, 43, 51; governmental control, 9; Indigenous, 28, 29; LMIC, direct service professionals in, 63–65

health expertise, 27, 41, 42, 69, 93, 101, 192–93; development practice, 27, 36, 46–49; health domain, 43–44; population health domain, 44–45, 48, 93; self-assessment of, 101; technical capabilities, 43–44

health information, 11

health insurance, 181

health policy and management, 43

health provider careers. *See* direct service careers

Health Volunteers Overseas, 65

HIC organizations: consultants, 27; funding, 30; move toward locally-led development, 30–37; as résumé target audience, 134

HIC professionals, 2, 3; cross-cultural work experiences, 75; direct service career paths, 63–64; impact of AIDS epidemic on, 10–11; in LMIC environments, 63–64; obstacles to global health careers, 75; overseas experience, 103

HICs. *See* high-income countries

high-income countries (HICs), 2, 3, 25; donor/implementation system, 14, 26, 27; international development role, 28–30; move toward locally-led development, 30–37. *See also* HIC organizations; HIC professionals

hiring managers, roles of: job interviewing, 172–73, 175–76, 179, 185; pre-interviewing, 168–69; résumé reviewing, 134–35, 136, 139–40, 142, 143–44, 151; salary negotiations, 185–86

hiring process, 38, 135; disorganized, 177; litigation related to, 171–72; timing, 176

Homentum, 34–35, 40

Horton, Robert, 29

humanitarian assistance, 43–44, 63, 64, 137, 153

human rights, 25, 43–44

Idealist website, 153

identity: gender, 44; of persons with disabilities, 45; professional, 2, 12, 44, 45; religious, 86, 87; student, 5, 95; team, 157

immunization programs, 9

implementation, of global health career strategies, 195–97. *See also* colleagues and coworkers; employers, potential; networking; online presence; professional records system

implementation science, 41, 67, 68–69. *See also* program implementation

Implementing Best Practices Consortium, 59

imposter syndrome, 82, 87, 109, 129

Indeed website, 153–54, 184

Indigenous communities, 28, 29

informational interviews, 19, 72, 169, 194, 196; differentiated from mentorship, 167; interpersonal interactions in, 156–57, 165–68

information flows, 59

information processing and technology, 42, 57. *See also* data analysis and management

inner observer, 16, 44–45, 158, 159, 193, 196; in career strategy foundation building, 81, 84–88; in compensation negotiations, 188; distinguished from inner critic, 88; in job interviews, 173–74, 177; as process, 130–31; relation to thought distortions, 88, 105, 113–14

innovation, 26, 58, 68, 98, 174–75, 176

Instagram, 146

Institute for Health Metrics and Evaluation, 92

internal job candidates, 174, 178

international development, 3, 75; academic preparation for, 70; culture of innovation, 58; definition, 2; donor funding, 25–27, 28; HIC/LMIC power differential, 30; history, 28–30, 63; job postings websites, 152–53; LMICs' professionals in, 30, 63. *See also* locally-led development

international health, definition, 23

International Medical Corps, 64

international organizations: accountability, 48; LMIC professionals in, 82; "market rates"-based salaries, 187; as potential employers, 93; project development approach, 69

Internet, 146; globalization and, 8–9, 11–12, 31, 53–54; as interview preparation tool, 171, 182–83; as job search tool, 19, 74, 93–94, 147, 152–54; as recruitment tool, 19, 137–38, 140, 146, 147, 152–54; as résumé and CV preparation tool, 133–34; role in knowledge access, 56, 70; role in locally-led development, 31

internships, 75, 168, 194

interviews, 57, 135; virtual, 157. *See also* informational interviews; job interviews; pre-interviews

intra- and interpersonal effectiveness, 9, 27, 42, 50, 56, 59, 101, 102–4, 103–4, 135, 188, 192–93, 195; components, 41; conflict-management skills, 173–74, 175; critical aspects, 50–53; deficits in, 70; in informational interviews, 156–57, 165–68; in job interviews, 165–66, 169–70, 173–74, 175–76; mindfulness component, 52–53, 59; in networking, 156–64; in pre-interviews, 165, 168–70, 188; recruiter's assessment, 135, 139; re-interview check of, 169–70; self-assessment, 101, 193

IntraHealth, 15

introvert personality, 112, 156–57, 157–58, 157–59

job change, 4

job descriptions, 149; key words, 134, 136, 137–39, 140–41, 171; matching skills with, 172–73; relation to cover letters, 144; on résumés, 131–32, 137, 138, 140–41

job interviews, 171–79, 188, 196; callbacks after, 179; interviewers' questions, 171–76, 178–79, 185; job candidates' questions, 176, 179; mistakes to avoid in, 176–79; post-interview etiquette, 179–80; red flags during, 177

job loss. *See* employment termination

job offers, 180; negotiations following, 170, 180–88

job postings websites, 73, 93, 102, 152–54, 153, 201–4

job satisfaction, 172

job search: critical best practices, 116, 191–92; knowledge management use in, 57; by new graduates, 72–73; online resources, 73, 93, 102, 152–54, 201–4; personal preferences and priorities in, 170–71, 180; psychological obstacles in, 5–6, 82–83, 95, 97; unsuccessful, 75–76, 82, 90

job shadowing, 194

job titles, 138, 149, 170–71, 196; salaries listed by, 184–85

Johns Hopkins University, 3, 11, 181

Johns Hopkins University Bloomberg School of Public Health, 54, 72, 86, 89, 181; Center for Communication Programs, 14–15, 60–61, 131

Jung, Carl, 158

Kaplan, Robert, 24

knowledge, attitudes, and behavior (KAB), 104

knowledge, attitudes, and practice (KAP), 3, 104

knowledge, attitudes, skills, and experiences (KASE), 3, 91, 193; potential employers' requirements, 102–4

knowledge, attitudes, skills, and experiences (KASE) gaps, 61; identification, 18, 99, 102–15, 116, 193; remediation, 116–23; review and self-rating, 101–2

knowledge hierarchies, 31, 34

knowledge management (KM), 40, 42, 51, 53, 67, 94, 100, 101, 192–93; components,

56–58; experts, 59; gap analysis of, 117; knowledge-doubling time concept, 56; self-assessment of, 101–4, 193
Kondo, Marie, 88

Ladders Inc., 135
Lancet, 29
Lancet Global Health Commission on High-Quality Health Systems in the SDG Era, 24
language skills, 102, 136, 144–45, 149
Latham, 117
LGBTQ+ rights, 33
LICs. *See* low-income countries (LICs)
Life Coaching School, 106
LifePlanningNetwork.org, 8
lifespan career considerations, 18, 20, 60–78, 192, 193–95, 196, 197. *See also* early career professionals; midcareer professionals; senior career professionals
LinkedIn/LinkedIn profiles, 12, 19, 84, 136, 146–53, 154, 195, 203; ATS/ARS searches, 148–49; control of full disclosure, 147, 148; endorsements on, 151, 164; keyword searches, 137–38, 148–50; as networking tool, 134, 152, 155, 157, 161, 164; photographs, 149; regular postings on, 151–52; Salary Insights, 184; updating, 147; URL link, 147, 148
LMIC professionals, 2, 3, 16, 25; direct service career paths, 63; domestically-based, 5, 9; domestic-to-global health transition, 10, 41, 73–75, 81–82, 83, 103; English language fluency, 144–45; expertise, 31, 34, 35, 36; fellowships, 135–36; in HIC-dominated environments, 7, 30, 91, 103; increase in overseas positions, 10; midcareer changes, 73–75; professional activism, 31–32; salary inequities, 7, 187; senior, 81–82; training, 31
LMICs. *See* lower- and middle-income countries
localization, 17, 26, 27–28, 36, 47, 69, 75
locally-led development, 27–37, 47, 103, 192; conditions for, 31–32; definition, 28, 31; impact on implementation career path, 69; obstacles to, 35–36; technology use in, 56; USAID support for, 27–28, 32–37.

See also capacity building and sustainability; decolonization; localization; reimagining
Locke, John, 96, 117
lower- and middle-income countries (LMICs), 2, 3, 9, 25; donor partnerships, 26–27; HIC-funded projects, 81; immunization programs, 9; lack of accountability, 30; medical students' practice in, 65; technology use, 37, 54, 56. *See also* LMIC professionals; locally-led development

MacArthur Foundation, 33
Macharia, Jennifer, 1–2, 72
malaria, 9–10, 29, 43
management skills, 51, 71, 90, 103, 175–76. *See also* project management
Martin, Keith, 10
master of public health (MPH)/master of health science (MHS): degrees and programs, 43, 70; graduates, 55–56, 66, 75, 82–83, 90
maternal and child health, 43, 44
Matthews, Gail, 120–21
medical schools and education, 63, 70
medical service careers. *See* direct service careers
meditation, 113
meetings, 50, 54, 159–60, 166, 171–72
mental imagery, 96
mentorship, 51, 72–73, 104, 156, 162–64, 167
M&E. *See* monitoring and evaluation
meta-analyses, 67
Microsoft Word, 134
midcareer professionals, 45, 60–61, 166; domestic-to-global career transitions, 13–17, 14–17, 23, 60–61, 62, 73–75, 166; fellowship programs, 16; professional records system, 128, 131
mindfulness, 52–53, 59, 84–85, 156
mindset, positive, 96
minority-serving institutions, 137
mistakes and failures, as job interview topic, 173
monitoring and evaluation (M&E), 37, 55, 66–68, 69, 71, 72
Monster online job board, 154

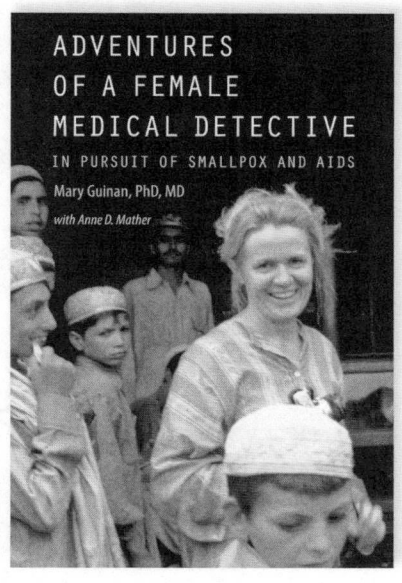
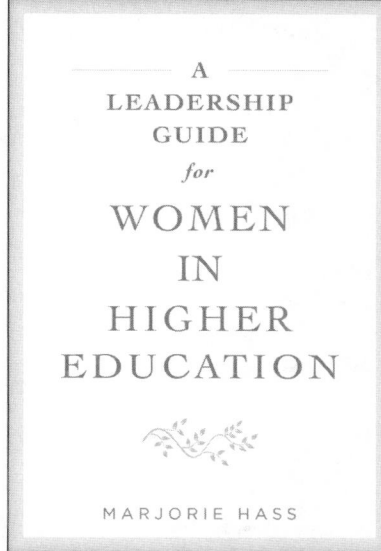
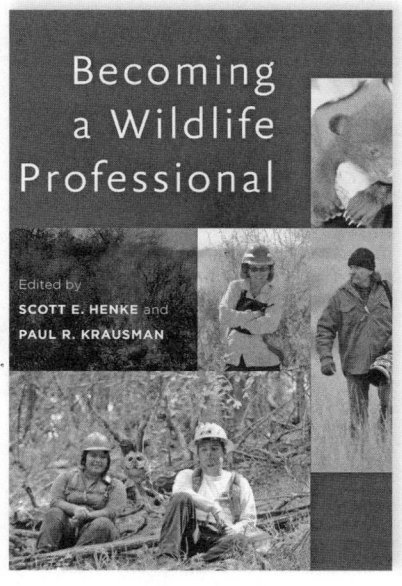
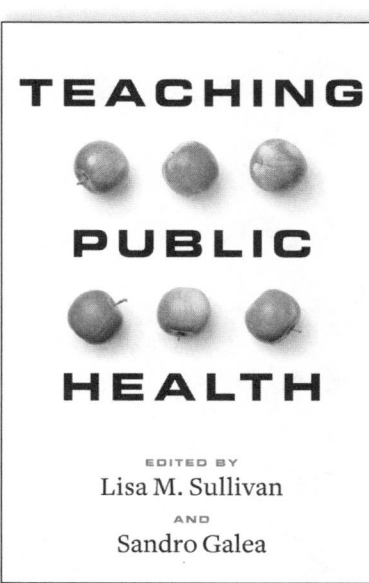